A. U. A. Language Center Thai Course

Reading & Writing Workbook
mostly writing

Prepared by
J. Marvin Brown

Southeast Asia Program Publications
Southeast Asia Program
Cornell University
Ithaca, New York
1997

Cornell Southeast Asia Program Publications
640 Stewart Avenue, Ithaca, NY 14850-3857

ISBN 978-0-87727-512-1

PREFACE

This WORKBOOK is meant to be used together with the TEXT of the AUA Reading and Writing Course. The Preface of the course, together with the Contents and Introduction, appear in the TEXT and won't be repeated here.

For ease of writing in a bound book, the Workbook sheets are printed horizontally and on one side only. And beginning with page 49, the sheets have been reversed. That is, after working *down* through the book to page 48, you then turn it over and work *up* from page 49 to the end.

J.M.B.

Bangkok, Thailand
December, 1979

1. THE SEVEN SONORANTS.

Practice copying the seven sonorants in the guidelines below. Use a small ruler to guide the long straight strokes. The purpose here is to build the shapes into your brain—not the movements into your fingers—and your copies should be perfect. Start with the loop in the direction indicated.

Now practice copying at normal handwriting size with guidelines but no ruler.

Now practice writing from memory. Look at the letter's name at the right and write it in the first column (far left). When you've finished the first column, cover it with your ruler and write the letters again in the second column, and so on.

ɲɔɔ ɲǔu

jɔɔ yák

ŋɔɔ wɛ̌ɛŋ

ŋɔɔ

lɔɔ liŋ

mɔɔ máa

rɔɔ

2. THE VOWEL aa.

Practice copying each of the following words directly under its model. Use a ruler for the large-scale copying.

Write each of the nonsense syllables (column 4) into column 1. Cover column 1 and write them again in 2. Then in 3. Next write Thai translations of the English words of column 7 into 5. Cover these and write again in 6.

1	2	3	4	5	6	7
			laaŋ			work
			maaw			long
			ŋaay			Mr.
			waa			Mrs.
			ŋaam			Laos
			raay			come
			waaw			long time
			raaŋ			watchman
			maay			take leave
			laan			medicine
			naa			yesterday
			raam			approx'ly
			waaŋ			rubber

2

3. THE VOWEL a.

Practice copying the three symbols in the guidelines below using a ruler. Then copy them together with nɔɔ nǔu.

Now practice copying the five symbols at normal size without a ruler. Use consonants as shown.

Now practice writing from memory. Follow the instructions given for the similar exercise of lesson 2. Use máy malay for sarà? ?ay in non-sense syllables. It is the more common of the two and can thus be called the regular one.

way	in
ŋaw	still
lam	dance
raŋ	it
ŋaaw	we

4. MEANINGFUL TEXT. (*Expansions*.)

Practice copying each of the following expressions directly under its model. Use a ruler for the large-scale copying.

ຂ້ອຍເປັນຄົນລາວ

ຫ້ອງການໃຫຍ່   ຫ້ອງການ   ຫ້ອງການໃຫຍ່ແທ້ແທ້ໃຫຍ່ແທ້ແທ້

Write in the parts of the reading exercise suggested by the English translations to the right.

Mr. Raan's watchman is still drunk.

Grandma May still comes to dance.

The Lao watchman came to report.

The watchman in our field is drunk.

Mr. Raan's field (it) is long.

Grandma May came to dance for a long time.

Miss Laos said goodbye to the boss.

Our watchman took a long leave from work.

Mr. Raan's watchman took leave from work.

Miss Laos still comes to dance.

4

5. THE SEVEN PLAIN STOPS.

Practice copying the seven plains in the guidelines below. Use a ruler for perfect copies.

Now practice copying the seven plains at normal handwriting size with guidelines but no ruler.

Now practice writing from memory. Proceed as with the corresponding exercise of lesson 1.

bɔɔ baymáay

ʔɔɔ ʔàaŋ

tɔɔ tàw

kɔɔ kày

dɔɔ dèk

pɔɔ plaa

cɔɔ caan

6. LONG DEAD SYLLABLES.

Go through the following steps for both of the stroke types given below. First trace the first line with a fixed rhythm to keep you at a certain speed (stroke, stroke, letter; stroke, stroke, letter; etc.). Next copy the whole line into the guidelines below it with the same rhythm. Then trace the next line rhythmically (stroke, letter; stroke, letter) and copy it into the guidelines below it. Finally, write the letters given in transcription, preceding each (rhythmically) with the stroke being practiced.

Practice writing from both transcriptions and English translations using the procedure described in lesson 2.

wâat	together
baaq	very
dam	die
ʔàap	go
kaw	mouth
daaw	plate
râap	take
baŋ	difficult
tàak	heart
bay	follow
lâat	from
ʔay	remember

9

7. SHORT DEAD SYLLABLES.

máy hǎn ʔaakàat must always be followed by a final consonant, and you might think of it as a link between the initial and final (the loop is above the initial and the end of the tail is above the final). Get a feeling for this linking vowel space in relation to the two consonants from the blocks given below. Let them guide you as you write the syllables given in transcription.

man   kàt   baŋ   lák   dàp   yaŋ

Now write, in the guidelines below, the syllables formed from the initials at the top and the finals at the left.

Practice writing from transcriptions, English translations, or both. Use the procedure described in lesson 2.

bite (kàt)	love
shy (ʔaay)	black
catch (càp)	in
drunk (maw)	day
receive (ráp)	long
temple (wát)	go
loud (daŋ)	follow
cough (ʔay)	mouth
steal (lák)	lâat
soft (baw)	nák
liver (tàp)	kam
arrange (càt)	yâap

8. MEANINGFUL TEXT. (*Expansions.*)

Write in translations of the following. Don't try for literal translations. Simply let the English remind you of the nearest equivalent in the reading exercise. Work across the page.

To be mean.	Very mean.	Our boss is very mean.
A pen.	Take a pen.	Bring the pen here and draw.
With Grandpa.	Make an appointment with Gr'pa.	Grandma and Grandpa made an appointment (to see each other).
Go to the Wat.	Take (it) to the Wat.	Take the pen to the Wat.
Hard to draw.	Very hard to draw.	It's very hard to draw a pen.
To love Grandma.	Grandpa loves Grandma.	Grandpa and Grandma love each other.
Follow us.	(It) followed us here.	(It) followed us here from the Wat.
Grandma Daaw.	Follow Grandma Daaw.	It followed after Grandma Daaw.
Still love.	We still love.	We still love Grandma Daaw.
It followed.	It followed the boss.	It followed after our boss.

8

9. THE SEVEN LOW ASPIRATES.

Practice copying the seven low aspirates in the guidelines below. Use a ruler.

Now practice copying at normal handwriting size with guidelines but no ruler.

Now practice writing from memory. Proceed as with the corresponding exercise of lesson 1.

thɔɔ thahǎan

fɔɔ fan

khɔɔ khwaay

sɔɔ sôo

hɔɔ nók hûuk

phɔɔ phaan

chɔɔ cháaŋ

10. THE VOWELS ɔɔ AND ɛɛ.

Go through the line below simply stroking from lower to upper dot. Then do it again, but make a loop before retracing each upstroke. Pause after the loop to keep it from influencing the upstroke.

Now copy sarà? ?ɛɛ from the first guidelines below into the second. Then copy both the vowel and its consonant into the third. Then do the same for mǎy malay and mǎy mǔan.

Practice writing from transcriptions, English translations, or both. Use the procedure described in lesson 2.

Eight.	Narrow (khɛɛp).	
To tell.	Gold (thɔɔŋ).	
Expensive.	Canal (khlɔɔŋ).	
Soi.	Tea (chaa).	
To do.	Word (kham).	
To like.	Far (klay).	
Red.	Teeth (fan).	
Fire.	Outside (nɔ̂ɔk).	
Cat.	Middle (klaaŋ).	
Enough.	phlâat.	
Hawaii.	khwaam.	
Fish.	khrɔ̂ɔp.	

10

The shapes, stroke order, and position relative to the consonant for sarà? ?ii and sarà? ?uu are shown to the right. In the large guidelines below, use a ruler to write sarà? ?ii above each consonant and sarà? ?uu below. In the first small-scale guidelines, trace the consonant, write sarà? ?ì? (without ruler), trace it again and write sarà? ?ù?. Do the same in the next set of guidelines with sarà? ?ii and sarà? ?uu. (Notice the left shift required with pɔɔ plaa and fɔɔ fan).

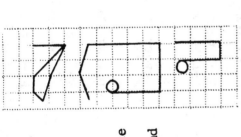

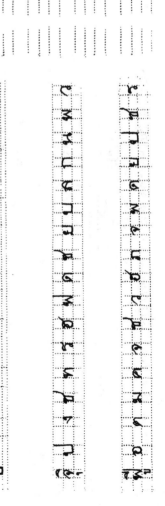

Practice writing from transcriptions, English translations, or both. Use the procedure described in lesson 2.

monkey (liŋ)		listen to
look at (duu)		to close
every (thúk)		to have
hurry (rîip)		mosquito
to eat (kin)		to do
more (?lík)		good
to chat (khúy)		to speak
clearly (chát)		cùt
to think (khít)		thuu
launder (sák)		puun

11

12. MEANINGFUL TEXT. (Expansions.)

Write the Thai suggested by the following English translations of the Thai text (proceed across).

Son.	Take (your) son.	Take (your) son to see (it).
In the canal.	Lie in the canal.	Water buffaloes like to lie in the canal.
Who with?	Who is (he) talking to?	Who is (your) son talking to?
Why?	Why (did he) go?	Why (did you) take the knife (with you)?
In the process of.	Is eating.	The cat is eating fish.
Grandma Phloy.	Tell Grandma Phloy.	Hurry and go tell Grandma Phloy.
Every time.	(He) looks at (me) every time.	Daeng likes to look at (me) every time.
Day time.	During the day.	(My) child sleeps during the day.
Again.	Tell (him) again.	Tell Uncle Chum again.
Go tell.	Hurry and go tell.	Hurry and go tell Uncle Chum.

12

13. THE SEVEN HIGH ASPIRATES.

Practice copying the seven high aspirates in the guidelines below. Use a ruler.

Now practice copying at normal handwriting size with guidelines but no ruler.

Now practice writing from memory. Proceed as with the corresponding exercise of lesson 1.

thɔ̌ɔ thǔŋ

fɔ̌ɔ fǎa

khɔ̌ɔ khày

sɔ̌ɔ sǔa

hɔ̌ɔ hlìp

phɔ̌ɔ phɛ̌ŋ

chɔ̌ɔ chìŋ

13

14. THE SEVEN 'HIGH SONORANTS'.

Practice making the heads of chɔɔ, sɔɔ, and khɔ̌ɔ. First make the single peak, then the double peak, and then alternations of the two.

Now practice the whole letters with a ruler.

Practice writing from transcriptions, English translations, or both. Use the procedure described in lesson 2.

Inject (chìit).	Sell.
Entrust (fàak).	Cheap.
Lonely (ŋǎw).	Thin.
Fancy (rǔuràa).	Ten.
Clear (sǎy).	Pork.
A cold (wàt).	Several.
Funny (khǎm).	Sweet.
Wrong (phìt).	Stop.
Tube (lɔ̀ɔt).	Disappear.
Guests (khɛ̀ɛk).	nǎy.

14

15. THE VOWELS e ee AND ɔ oo.

The shapes and positions of saraʔ ʔoo and máy tày khúu are shown to the right. (They are placed around the same consonant simply to save space. They never occur together like this.) rɔɔ rɯa is also sketched in lightly to show how it compares with sarà? ?oo. Copy the letters given at the beginning of each set of guidelines below in the order sarà? ?oo, consonant, máy tày khúu. Change the consonant if you like.

Practice writing from transcriptions, English translations, or both. Use the procedure described in lesson 2.

To be (pen).			Rain.
All gone (mòt).			Seven.
Little (lék).			To see.
To descend (loŋ).			O'clock.
By oneself (ʔeeŋ).			Six.
World (lôok).			Hair, I.
Full (tem).			People.
Bird (nók).			Fast.
By (dooy).			To keep.
Time (weelaa).			ʔèek.

15

16. MEANINGFUL TEXT. (*Short dialogs.*)

Write the Thai suggested by the following English translations of the Thai text.

Uncle ate mackerel.

....

When did Uncle
eat mackerel?

....

Uncle ate mackerel
in the late morning.

....

The children went
to a show.

....

When did the children
go to a show?

....

The children
went to a show while
it was raining.

....

Nephew
sold sweet pork.

....

When did Nephew
sell sweet pork?

....

Nephew sold sweet
pork in the evening.

....

The teacher went
to see the doctor.

....

Why did the teacher go
to see the doctor?

....

The teacher
had a cold.

....

(My) son is a doctor.

.... The doctor is a Chinese.

(My) daughter is a teacher.

.... The farmer is a Lao.

(My) nephew is a sales clerk.

.... The teacher is a Korean.

(My) niece is a secretary.

.... The sales clerk is an Indian.

16

17. REVIEW BY NONSENSE SYLLABLES.

Writing unmarked tones with plain initials is easy (there's only one possible unmarked tone for each type and only one way of writing it). But with aspirates and sonorants there are always two possible unmarked tones and you have the constant problem of choosing the correct one of two consonant possibilities to show the tone you want. To get practice making these choices, go through the following steps (you could profitably practice doing this for hours). 1) Select a sound from the initial chart (top center). 2) Proceed along one of the three arrows selecting one of the two tones along the way. 3) Select one of the finals from the chart at the end of the arrow. 4) Write the syllable in the space to the right (and on extra paper).

Initial chart:

```
kh ch th ph f s h
ŋ  n  m  y  r  l w
```

Top right finals chart:

```
-aak -aat -aap
-ɔɔk -ɔɔt -ɔɔp
-ɛɛk -ɛɛt -ɛɛp
-iik -iit -iip
-uuk -uut -uup
-eek -eet -eep
-ook -oot -oop
```

Middle right finals chart:

```
-ak -at -ap
-ik -it -ip
-uk -ut -up
-ek -et -ep
-ok -ot -op
```

Bottom finals chart:

```
-aa -aaŋ -aan -aam -aay -aaw
    -aŋ  -an  -am  -ay  -aw
-ɔɔ -ɔɔŋ -ɔɔn -ɔɔm -ɔɔy
    -ɔŋ  -ɔn  -ɔm  -ɔy
-ɛɛ -ɛɛŋ -ɛɛn -ɛɛm      -ɛɛw
    -ɛŋ  -ɛn  -ɛm       -ɛw
-ii      -iin -iim      -iw
    -iŋ  -in  -im
-uu -uuŋ -uun -uum -uy
    -uŋ  -un  -um
-ee -eeŋ -een -eem      -eew
    -eŋ  -en  -em       -ew
-oo -ooŋ -oon -oom -ooy
    -oŋ  -on  -om
```

17

18. REVIEW BY WORDS.

Write (on extra paper) the Thai words for the following English 'translations'. Don't expect the English to be accurate or complete. It is only intended to *remind* you of the Thai words on page 18 of the Text. Check those words that give you difficulty and write them again.

middle	canal	to like	period	every time	close	look at	mosquito	world	doctor
bite	buffalo	clear	cut	mackerel	to be	it	cool	temple	pig
together	words	tea	eyes	birds	eight	come	separate	day	back
with	think	male	follow	outside	to go	very	love	time	nephew
eat	chat	wipe	die	lie down	I (m)	to have	dance	two	sweet
keep	narrow	Soi	attach	appointment	thin	knife	hurry	three	look for
curry	who	launder	hit	to count	rain	drunk	fast	late morn	rock
far	work	trap	full	rice field	meet	cat	we	ten	ears
ask for	grab	black	ask	Mrs.	enough	o'clock	down	color	see
legs	from	pencil	sack	a minute	fan	yet	wind	tall	iron
sell	plate	good	cheap	long time	1,000	how	take leave	orange	where
white	remember	look	gold	Mr.	take	medicine	Lao	100,000	bathe
Indians	Chinese	suck	way	in	speak	difficult	monkey	six	more
arms	seven	children	'slash'	on	ex'sive	rubber	uncle	thick	again
people	heart	red	to do	tell	listen	watchman	child	cold	1 (in 21)
yes (m)	mean	by	a time	fish	teeth	grandma	little	mouse	AUA
teacher	shine	straight	every	mouth	fire	long	secretary	all gone	take

18

19. ALPHABETICAL ORDERING. (*The first two positions.*)

Alphabetize each of the four lists below by steps. 1) Write the 1st position symbol (the first consonant) after each word (1st column of spaces). 2) Order these consonants in the second column and complete each word. 3) Write the 2nd position symbol after each word (3rd column). 4) Use these symbols to order words having the same first consonant and write final ordering in the 4th column.23*

20. MEANINGFUL TEXT. (*Jane's and Phloy's families.*)

Write the following in Thai.

Write the following questions (in the first lines) and their answers (in the second).

Mrs. Jane is a Canadian.

....

Her husband is a Chinese.

....

They have two sons

and three daughters.

....

Mrs. Phloy is a Thai.

....

Her husband is a Korean.

They have three sons

and two daughters.

....

Mrs. P and her 3 sons

took Mrs. J and her

....

3 daughters to a show.

Mrs. J's husband and sons

....

took Mrs. P's husband and

daughters to the beach.

....

Where did the sons
of the Thai go?

....

Where did the daughters
of the Korean go?

....

Where did the sons
of the Chinese go?

....

Where did the daughters
of the Canadian go?

....

Where did the daughters
of the Thai go?

....

Where did the sons
of the Korean go?

....

Where did the daughters
of the Chinese go?

....

20

21. máy ʔèek.

Practice writing the following common expressions. Note that the question particle máy is written máy (compare this with kháw, written khǎw on page 20 of the Text.)

Practice writing from transcriptions, English translations, or both.

Thai	Transliteration	English
....	khwâm.	Skillful (kèŋ).
....	Chicken.	Iron (lèk).
....	Eight.	Clf of books (lêm).
....	Enough.	Ring (wɛ̌ɛn).
....	Father.	Eyeglasses (wɛ̂n).
....	Speak.	Break (tɛ̀ɛk).
....	A little.	Ma'am (mɛɛm).
....	To sit.	A box (klɔ̀ŋ).
....	Afternoon.	A space (chɔ̂ŋ).
....	To send.	Handsome (lɔ̀ɔ).
....	Cheap.	To be full (ʔìm).
....	To order.	Young man (nùm).
....	More than.	nûm.

22. DOUBLE INITIAL CONSONANTS.

Write the following words twice each.

Write the four words of each group (in the order indicated) in the guidelines to the right.

Want.	Stink (mɛ̌n).	1 nǔu 3 nɔɔn 2 nfi 4 nàay	
Return.	Turn (mǔn).	ŋáa ŋáay ŋɔ̌ɔn ŋuu	
To be at.	All gone (mòt).	thfi thaaŋ thǔu thàan	
Pig.	More than (kwàa).	wɔɔn wàaŋ wǐi wâaŋ	
Straight.	Odor (klìn).	sǔuŋ sìi sǎam sɔɔy	
Kind of.	Young man (nùm).	yɔɔn yaaŋ yǐi yâam	
Right side.	Strange (plɛ̀ɛk).	phfi phɔɔm phàan phɔ̌ɔm	
Which?	Eyeglasses (wɛ̂n).	lâaŋ lùu lɔɔy làay	
New.	Pillow (mɔ̌ɔn).	khiim khɔ̌ɔŋ khùu khâay	
Far.	Ma'am (mɛ̂m).	mii mùu mâan mɔ̌ɔn	
To sit.	Sweep (kwàat).	fàay fɔɔŋ fùuŋ fâam	
To play.	Heavy (nàk).	rìi ràa râaŋ ruu	

23. THE VOWELS ía AND ua.

Before you write each word, compose it in your mind: see first the initial or cluster (being especially mindful of hɔ̌ɔ nam) and then the vowel formed around it. Then copy left to right from your mind's picture. Don't leave a space between the words of the two-word phrases.

Yellow.
Hate
(klìat).
Visit friends
(yɛ̂am phɤ̂an).

Study.
Almost
(kùap).
To compare
(prìap thîap).

Salt.
Sound
(sìaŋ).
Furniture
(khrɤ̂aŋ rɯan).

Write.
Story
(rɤ̂aŋ).
Writing implements
(khrɤ̂aŋ khǐan).

Believe.
Quiet
(ŋîap).
Northeast
(chǐaŋ nɯa).

Noon.
Tired
(nɯ̀ay).
Sound of friends
(sìaŋ phɤ̂an).

Month.
Change
(plìan).
Unbelievable
(lɯa chɯ̂a).

Green.
Visit
(yɛ̂am).
Go boating
(thîaw rɯa).

Friend.
klaw.
Sound of calling
(sìaŋ rîak).

To call.
khrɤ̂aŋ.
Like friends
(mɯan phɤ̂an).

Boat.
thîaw.
Change the sound
(plìan sìaŋ).

23

24. MEANINGFUL TEXT. *(Jane's and Phloy's families, continued.)*

Write the following in Thai. Write, also, the answers to the questions.

Mr. Kim Liang is Mrs. Jane's husband. ....

He's been in Thailand for 18 years. ....

He's a barber and works in Banglampoo. ....

Mr. Soon Muk Chung is Mrs. Phloy's husband. ....

He's been in Thailand for 6 months. ....

He's a mechanic and works at Don Muang. ....

How long has Mr. Kim Liang been in Thailand? ....

Where does Mrs. Phloy's husband work? ....

Whose husband is the barber? ....

How many daughters has the Korean got? ....

How long has the husband of the Thai
been in Thailand? ....
Where does the father of the two sons work? ....

The one who's been in Thailand for 6 months;
whose husband is he? ....
How many daughters
has the one who works in Banglampoo got? ....
The mother of the three sons is the Thai, right? ....

24

25. máy thoo.

Falling tones with aspirate and sonorant initials can be written either with low consonants plus máy ʔèek (L1) or high consonants plus máy thoo (H2), and actual spellings must be memorized. The special symbol ~ is introduced below to distinguish H2 (~) from L1 (^).

Practice writing the following expressions.

Expression	Meaning	Meaning
	Give.	Port (thâa).
	Already.	If (thâa).
	Can.	Ought (nâa).
	Use.	Face (nâa).
	House.	Father (phɔ̂ɔ).
	Near.	Mother (mɛ̂ɛ).
	Wood.	Enter (khâw).
	Shirt.	Rice (khâaw).
	Morning.	Cloth (phâa).
	Nine.	Know (rúu).
	Far.	Must (tɔ̂ŋ).

25

26. THE VOWELS ึ, ืม, ัว, AND ัว.

Practice writing the following expressions.

Write the following words twice each.

Expression	Word
Go up.	Have ever (khəəy)
Help.	Also (dûay)
Walk.	Ink (mùk)
One.	Question (lɛ̌ɛ)
Head.	Bee (phʉ̂ŋ)
10,000.	Depend on (phʉ̂ŋ)
Or.	At all (ləəy)
Bottle.	Late (dʉ̀k)
Forget.	Name (chʉ̂ʉ)
Pretty.	Whiskers (nùat)
To buy.	Massage (nûat)
Open.	Think (nʉ́k)
Hand.	Kitchen (khrua)

26

27. 'GLOTTAL' VOWELS.

Syllables are written in transcription below without tones. Write each of these with whichever tones you know how to write under the appropriate tone marker to the right of the transcription.32* Notice that all syllables are dead, so no mid or rising tones are possible.

	ˊ	ˇ	ˋ		ˊ	ˇ	ˋ
chʉʉt				wɛʔ			phloʔ
ŋat				chook			kʉap
leʔ				nep			fʉk
mot				yeʔ			keet
ʔʉʔ				suup			cəʔ
riit				phluaʔ			dek
yuʔ				riak			phiaʔ
thaɛk				phraʔ			lɛɛk
dup				pɛɛt			paʔ
siʔ				ʔok			hit
maak				cɔʔ			tɔɔp

27

28. MEANINGFUL TEXT. (Somchai's family.)

Here is the story in both transcription and translation. Write the story in Thai (on a separate sheet of paper) from the transcription (which gives writing hints when the spelling doesn't correspond exactly with the pronunciation). Then try to write the story from the translation. Refer to the transcription when you run up against translation difficulties.

Mr. Somchai is a barber. He works at a barbershop near the Indra Hotel. He's married and has three children, but his parents and brothers and sisters all live upcountry. He's got an older brother, an older sister, a younger brother, and a younger sister.

His older brother is a doctor and works in Chiang Mai. He's married and has ten children.

His older sister is a teacher and teaches at a school in Songkhla. She's also married but hasn't got any children yet. Her husband is a businessman.

The two younger ones are still students, and they live with their parents in Nong Khai province. The younger brother wants to be a doctor like his older brother, but the younger sister wants to be a dressmaker.

Somchai's father is a farmer. His mother is a vendor. She goes out and sells things every day.

Every year during the cold season, Mr. Somchai goes home to see his parents and younger brother and sister in Nong Khai. But he hasn't seen his older brother or sister for almost five years now because they don't get along very well.

naay sŏmchaay pen châŋ tàt phŏm. kháw (ˇ)
tham ŋaan thîi ráan tàt phŏm klâyklây rooŋrɛɛm
ʔinthraa. kháw (ˋ) tɛ̀ŋŋaan lɛ́ʔ mii lûuk sǎam khon
lɛ́ɛw, tɛ̀ɛ phɔ̂ɔ mɛ̂ɛ phîi nɔ́ɔŋ khɔ̌ɔŋ (ɔ̌ɔ) kháw (ˇ)
yùu tâaŋ caŋwàt thaŋnan. kháw (ˇ) mii phîi chaay
khon nɯŋ (ˋ), phîi sǎaw khon nɯŋ (ˋ), nɔ́ɔŋ chaay
khon nɯŋ, lɛ́ʔ nɔ́ɔŋ sǎaw khon nɯŋ.

phîi chaay kháw pen mɔ̌ɔ. tham ŋaan yùu thîi
chiaŋmày. tɛ̀ŋŋaan lɛ́ɛw lɛ́ʔ mii lûuk sìp khon.

phîi sǎaw pen khruu. sɔ̌ɔn yùu thîi rooŋrian
nay caŋwàt sɔ̌ŋkhlǎa. tɛ̀ŋŋaan lɛ́ɛw mɯ̌ankan, tɛ̀ɛ
yaŋ mây mii lûuk. sǎamii kháw pen phɔ̂ɔ kháa.

nɔ́ɔŋ sɔ̌ɔŋ khon yaŋ pen nákrian yùu, lɛ́ʔ yùu
kàp phɔ̂ɔ mɛ̂ɛ thîi caŋwàt nɔ̌ɔŋkhaay. nɔ́ɔŋ chaay
yàak ca (àʔ) pen mɔ̌ɔ mɯ̌an phîi chaay, tɛ̀ɛ nɔ́ɔŋ
sǎaw yàak ca (àʔ) pen châŋ tàt sɯ̂a.

phɔ̂ɔ khɔ̌ɔŋ (ɔ̌ɔ) naay sɒ̌mchaay pen chaawnaa.
mɛ̂ɛ pen mɛ̂ɛ kháa. ʔɔ̀ɔk pay khǎay khɔ̌ɔŋ thúk wan.

thúkthúk pii tɔɔn nǎa nǎaw, naay sŏmchaay klàp
pay hǎa phɔ̂ɔ mɛ̂ɛ lɛ́ʔ nɔ́ɔŋ thîi nɔ̌ɔŋkhaay. tɛ̀ɛ
kháw mây dâay phóp phîi tháŋ sɔ̌ɔŋ khon kɯ̀ap hǎa pii
lɛ́ɛw, phrɔ́ʔ wâa kháw mây khǒy thùuk kan.

28

29. WEAK SYLLABLES.

The problem in *writing* weak syllables is when to write sarà? ?à? and when not to. The following suggestion will at least help you guess. *Whenever the second syllable has a sonorant initial that would require hɔ́ɔ nam, try to get the consonant of the first syllable to do the job. In all other cases use the low consonant (but high for s) with* sarà? ?à?. Notice how much easier the second (correct) spelling is in the examples below.

thanŏn	phanăŋ	khanàat	sawăaŋ	talàat
ถนน	พนัง	คนาด	สว่าง	ตลาด
ถนน	พนัง	คนาด	สว่าง	ตลาด

When the weak syllable is kra, pra, or tra, the above suggestion does not apply. You *must* use sarà? ?à? and sarà? ?ù?. And when you hear words beginning with ka or pa, more often than not they will be cases of kra or pra spoken in non-standard Thai.

The only other vowels that occur in weak syllables of this type are i and u. They are written with sarà? ?i? and sarà? ?ú?. These will always lose the glottal stop when spoken, but only occasionally the tone (phíseet, but ?isăan; thurian, but burìi).

Write the following words. They are chosen so that the above advice will always be right.

sanɔ̀?, sadùak
sanàp sanŭn

sa?àat, sawěey
samăm saměe

khayěŋ, khanɛɛn
khayà? khayěɛŋ

chamát, chalìa
chawàt chawĭan

thayɛɛŋ, thanàt
thalěe thalǎy

phanàŋ, phanɛɛk
pha?ùut pha?om

talìŋ, talɔ̀ɔt
takuy takaay

camùuk, carùat
?arèt ?arɔy

?aràam, ?anèek
?alúm ?alùay

kramɔ̀m, kradaan
kraprĭi krapràw

pralàat, pramàa
pradàp pradaa

wílay, ?isăan
phíthĭi phíthăn

kulàap, thúrian
surǐy surăay

29

30. SYLLABLE BOUNDARIES.

Syllables are written in transcription below without tones. Write each of these with whichever tones you know how to write under the appropriate tone marker to the right of the transcription. Remember that aspirates and sonorants have two ways of writing falling tones. Write both.

	ˇ	ˊ	ˋ	—		ˇ	ˊ	ˋ	—
mɯɯn					wiŋ				
piin					deen				
thum					nɯaŋ				
ŋua					bon				
kɛ(ɛ)m					suan				
phlee					nen				
rooŋ					ʔɛɛ				
ʔɛɛ					khe(e)ŋ				
faaŋ					yɔ(ɔ)m				
luay					tam				
cuuŋ					chiaŋ				
hey									

30

31. SPECIAL TONES.

máy trii is really the Thai numeral 7, but as a tone marker it is rarely called lêek cèt (as máy tày khǔu is sometimes called lêek pɛ̀ɛt). For each size below, write máy trii in the first line and alternate it with máy tày khǔu in the second.

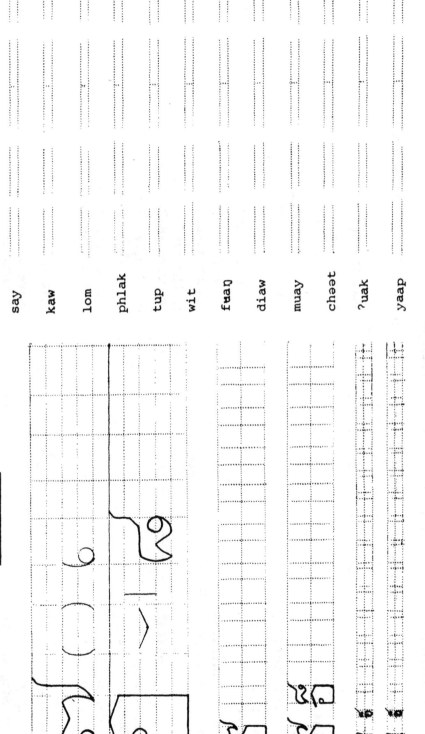

Syllables are written in transcription below without tones. Write the 5 or 6 possible tones for live syllables and the 2 *main* tones for each dead. (If you choose to write *all 3* dead tones, put the *far out* ones in parentheses.)

	ˇ	´	ˆ	ˋ	‐
say					
kaw					
lom					
phlak					
tup					
wit					
fɯaŋ					
diaw					
muay					
cheat					
ʔuak					
yaap					

31

32. MEANINGFUL TEXT. *(Somchai's family, continued.)*

Write the following questions and their answers in Thai (on the same line).

What is Sanoh? .... What is Pracuap? ....

Where does
Chalaem live? ....

Has Chaliaw got
any children yet? ....

Is Samaan
married yet? ....

How many children
has Chalaem got? ....

Has Pracuap got
any children yet? ....

Is Chaluay
married yet? ....

How many children
has Chaluay got? ....

Where does
Sanoh live? ....

What is Sangiam? ....

Is Chaliaw
married yet? ....

Where does
Chaliaw live? ....

Has Sangiam got
any children yet? ....

Is Sanoh
married yet? ....

How many children
has Somchai got? ....

Has Chalaem got
any children yet? ....

What is Chaluay? ....

How many children
has Sangiam got? ....

Where does
Samaan live? ....

Where does
Pracuap live? ....

Has Sanoh got
any children yet? ....

What does Samaan
want to be? ....

How many children
has Chaliaw got? ....

33. THE SEVEN COMMON IRREGULARS.

Practice copying the seven common irregulars in the guidelines below. Use a ruler.

Now practice copying at normal handwriting size with guidelines but no ruler.

Now practice writing from memory. Proceed as with the corresponding exercise of lesson 1.

phɔɔ sǎmphaw

nɔɔ neen

sɔ̌ɔ ruusǐi

khɔɔ rakhaŋ

sɔ̌ɔ sǎalaa

yɔɔ yǐŋ

thɔɔ thoŋ

33

34. IRREGULAR FINALS.

Practice copying the common expressions given below (left). Then practice writing them from memory (right). Note mistakes in one column and then cover that column as you try again in the next.

สวัสดี	Hello.
ขอบคุณ	Thanks.
ขอโทษ	Excuse me.
คุณครับ	Sir? Ma'am?
กรุงเทพ	Bangkok.
ภาษาไทย	Thai.
ประเทศไทย	Thailand.
ภาคอาคาร	Restaurant.
ผู้หญิง	Women.
ร้อยบาท	100 baht.
อาจจะ	Might.
ควรจะ	Should.

34

35. SILENT FINALS.

Practice copying the common expressions given below (left). Memorize the spellings and practice writing them (right). *(Notice the special spelling for 'newspaper'.)*

รถยนต์	....	....	Automobile.
กระดาษ	....	....	Paper.
โทรศัพท์	....	....	Telephone.
ราชประสงค์	....	....	Rajaprasong.
ธนาคาร	....	....	Bank.
ไปรษณีย์	....	....	Post office.
สุขุมวิท	....	....	Sukhumvit.
หนังสือพิมพ์	....	....	Newspaper.
สถานทูต	....	....	Embassy.
วันอาทิตย์	....	....	Sunday.
อังคาร พุธ	....	....	Tues, Wed.
ศุกร์ เสาร์	....	....	Fri, Sat.

35

36. MEANINGFUL TEXT. (*Somchai's family*, continued.)

Write the following questions and their answers in Thai. Use the first four as models.

khun chalǔay ʔaw naŋsɯ̌ɯphim pay praysanii
wan nǎy.   ....

wan sǎw khun sanǒ? ʔaw bia pay nǎy.   ....

wan ʔathít khray ʔaw rótyon pay râatprasɔ̌ŋ.   ....

wan phút khun chalǐaw ʔaw ʔaray pay thanakhaan.   ....

Where did Khun Chaluay take the newspaper
on Friday?   ....

What did Khun Chalaem take to Rajaprasong
on Sunday?   ....

Who took the newspaper to the Post Office
on Friday?   ....

On what day did Khun Chalaem take the car
to Rajaprasong?   ....

Where did Khun Sangiam take the paper
on Tuesday?   ....

What did Khun Chaluay take to the Post Office
on Friday?   ....

On what day did Khun Sanoh take the beer
to the Erawan Hotel?   ....

Who took the paper to the Embassy on Tuesday?   ....

37. REVIEW BY NONSENSE SYLLABLES.

Memorize and practice writing the following lines. They include all the vowels and provide a convenient way of remembering them. Notice that there are 12 longs, 12 shorts, and 12 glottals (with sarà ʔàʔ appearing twice). 42*

Use the most probable spelling as you write the following words and then check actual spellings in the note. 43*

เดราจนำไรเปืดเดื่อดแมน๋อ The 9 regular longs.

เชอหนายคน ปวคทง กนรย The 3 irregular longs.

เพาะใช้ผู้หนายล่าวา The 7 short a's.

ก็นรอดดันหหนู The 5 other shorts.

เพาระโทะเทะกะระเยอเนะ The 6 normal glottals.

อีด   เอียะ เวือะ อัว The 6 other glottals.

The sec'y has been at the school for 2 months now.

She used to walk, get headaches, forget her name.

They won't let Farangs do it

as far as 76 feet

because of the many tables in the way.

ʔìʔ ʔìʔ ʔùʔ, ʔìaʔ ʔìaʔ ʔùaʔ

kramòm	....	kratɔ́ɔp
khayàw	....	prachót
ʔaŋun	....	chamát
pralàat	....	sathɔ́ɔn
chanòot	....	chaŋèe
camùuk	....	krapɔ̌ɔŋ
khayàʔ	....	krahǎay
krayɓ̀ɔŋ	....	kranɛ̌ɛ
thalɛ̀ŋ	....	samɛ̌ɛ
chalɛ̂m	....	ʔaray
krarɔ̀ɔk	....	ʔarɔ̀y
chaŋɓ̀ok	....	ʔalǔm ʔalùay

37

Write (on extra paper) the Thai words for the following English 'translations'. Don't expect the English to be accurate or complete. It is only intended to *remind* you of the Thai words on page 38 of the Text. Check those words that give you difficulty and write them again.

too, then	near	kitchen	tailor	must	noon	butter
paper	chicken	should	beach	need	telephone	over there
Bangkok	ask for	particle?	name	upcountry	Thai	yonder
box	excuse me	particle	morning	cabinet	bank	some
camera	thanks	Mr Mrs Miss	invite	dance	business	baht
more than	side	typewriter	that's so	kick	sit	afternoon
before	upstairs	sleepy	use	short	there	cigarette
how many	downstairs	will	left	table	that	number
shrimps	in front of	particle	particle	road	water	beer
February	go up	particle?	buy	reach	blue	divide
skillful	he she they	province	also, too	get along	sugar	door
salt	enter	kind of	as	throw away	a little bit	country
nine	understand	help	walk	place, at	fingers	ache
chair	brush off	spoon	single	only	here	jungle
island	write	slow	can	how much	this	aunt
glass	green	barber	market	feet	think	papa

grandfather	special	twenty	below	embassy	a little	give
not, empty	older sib	borrow	million	field	book	new
change	Wednesday	lots	forget	comfortable	newspaper	American
percent	Ploenchit	car	number (cardinal)	soap	face	America
open	just now	motor car	number (ordinal)	toilet	window	want
post office	goat	sing	play	pretty	cold season	kind of
cloth	language	hot	at all	hello	one	be at
person	limes	hundred	turn	order	10,000	fat
man	dark	between	and then	notice	or	what
woman	hands	Rajathewi	and	short	a room	Tuesday
a sheet of	mosquito net	Rajaprasong	traffic circle	husband	bathroom	might
side	clouds	shop	cow	important	head	professor
Burma	wife	restaurant	(say) that	four	five	Sunday
syllable	mother	know s'thing	Vietnam	Sukhumvit	North	read
Paholyothin	vendor	know s'one	Saladaeng	polite	like	food
father	not	call	Friday	shirt	liquor	Erawan
businessman	wood	study	zero	put	yellow	opportunity
print	match	school	send	female	dry	Hong Kong

39. ALPHABETICAL ORDERING. (All positions.)

For each group of words below, 1) write (in the circle) the *number of the first position where the words of the group differ;* 2) write (in the spaces following the circle) the *letters in that position for each word,* and 3) number the words (in the spaces preceding them) according to the *relative order of these letters.* The first group is done as an example.

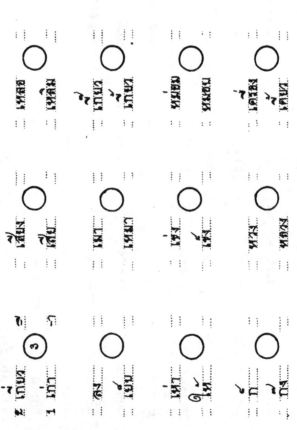

Copy out ten words at a time *in random order* from pages 38-39 of the Text and alphabetize them relative to each other. Then look them up in a dictionary.

40. MEANINGFUL TEXT. (*The Three Bears.*)

Write the story from the transcription.

mǐi kàp dèk nɔ́ɔy

naan maa lɛ́ɛw mii rɨaŋ thîi kìaw kàp khrɔ́ɔp-
khrua mǐi khrɔ́ɔpkhrua nɨŋ. mii yùu dûaykan sǎam
tua, khɨɨ phɔ̂ɔ, mɛ̂ɛ, lɛ́ʔ lûuk. cháaw wan nɨŋ
mɛ̂ɛ mǐi tham khâaw tôm pen ʔaahǎan cháaw. mɨ̂a
tham lɛ́ɛw, kɔ̂ tàk sáy chaam wáy sǎam chaam, khɨɨ
chaam bay yày khɔ̌ɔŋ phɔ̂ɔ, chaam bay klaaŋ khɔ̌ɔŋ
mɛ̂ɛ, lɛ́ʔ chaam bay lék khɔ̌ɔŋ lûuk. tɛ̀ɛ mǐi thaŋ
sǎam kɔ̂ yaŋ kin khâaw tôm mây dâay phrɔ́ʔ khâaw
tôm yaŋ rɔ́ɔn yùu. mɛ̂ɛ mǐi cɨŋ chuan phɔ̂ɔ mǐi
kàp lûuk mǐi ʔɔ̀ɔk pay dəɛn lên nɔ̂ɔk bâan kɔ̀ɔn,
phɨ̂a ca khɔɔy hây khâaw yen loŋ nɔ̀y, lɛ́ɛw ca
klàp maa kin kan.

nay weelaa thîi phɔ̂ɔ mǐi, mɛ̂ɛ mǐi, lɛ́ʔ lûuk
mǐi ʔɔ̀ɔk pay dəɛn lên nán, kɔ̂ mii dèk yǐŋ lék-
lék khon nɨŋ chɨɨ cǔmcim dəɛn phàan maa thaaŋ
bâan khɔ̌ɔŋ mǐi dây klîn ʔaahǎan. kháaw cɨŋ dəɛn
kháaw pay ʔɛ̀ɛp duu thaaŋ nâatàaŋ, kɔ̂ hěn mii
ʔaahǎan yùu bon tóʔ sǎam chaam, tɛ̀ɛ mây hěn mii
khon yùu ləəy. kháaw kɔ̂ ləəy pəət pratuu khâaw
pay nay bâan lɛ́ʔ rîip dəɛn troŋ pay thîi tóʔ
ʔaahǎan. phɔɔ pay thɨ̌ŋ tóʔ, kháaw kɔ̂ tàk khâaw
tôm nay chaam bay yày chim kɔɔn,

41

tὲε man róon keen pay. kháw kó tὲk kháaw tôm nay
chaam bay klaaŋ chim báaŋ, tὲε man yen keen pay.
kháw leey pay chim kháaw tôm nay chaam lέk, ruusὲk
wάa man kamlaŋ dii kó leey kin con con mòt chaam.

phoo kin kháaw lέεw, cὕmcὕm kó ruusὲk yὰak nάŋ
phák, kó hĕn mii káw?ti yùu sǎam tua. kháw looŋ
pay nάŋ thfi tua yày kòon, tὲε man sǔuŋ keen pay.
kháw looo pay nάŋ thfi tua klaaŋ, tὲε man kó tfa
keen pay ?lik. kháw kó leey deen pay nάŋ thfi tua
lέk, ruusὲk wάa nάŋ dΰay phoo dii lέεw kó sabaay
dΰay, leey nάŋ yùu naan con káw?ti hák.

mΰa káw?ti hák, kháw cὕŋ lúk khân lέ? deen
kháw pay nay hôŋ noon. mooŋ hĕn tiaŋ yùu sǎam
tiaŋ. kháw kó khân pay noon bon tiaŋ yày kòon,
tὲε noon mάy sabaay phro? man khΰŋ keen pay.
kháw leey khân pay noon bon tiaŋ klaaŋ, kó ruusὲk
mάy sabaay ?lik phro? man nΰm keen pay. kháw cὕŋ
looŋ khân pay noon bon tiaŋ lέk, kó ruusὲk sabaay
dii, lέεw kháw kó leey làp pay.

phoo dèk yĭŋ cὕmcὕm noon làp pay lέεw, mii
thaŋ sǎam tua kó klàp maa thΰŋ báan. thaŋ sǎam

troŋ khâw pay thîi tɔ́ ʔaahǎan. phɔɔ thɯ̌ŋ tɔ́,
phɔɔ mǐi kɔ̂ phûut sǐaŋ daŋ wâa 'mii khray maa kin
khâaw tôm khɔ̌ŋ chǎn.' mɛ̂ɛ mǐi kɔ̂ phûut wâa 'mii
khray maa kin khâaw tôm khɔ̌ŋ chǎn mǔankan.' lûuk
mǐi kɔ̂ phûut wâa 'mii khray maa kin khâaw tôm
khɔ̌ŋ nǔu mǔankan, lɛ́ɛw kɔ̂ kin khɔ̌ŋ nǔu mòt lǝǝy.'

phɔɔ mǐi cɯŋ deen pay duu thîi kâwʔîi lɛ́ɛw kɔ̂
phûut sǐaŋ daŋ wâa, 'mii khray maa nâŋ thîi kâwʔîi
chǎn.' mɛ̂ɛ mǐi kɔ̂ phûut wâa, 'mii khray maa nâŋ
thîi kâwʔîi chǎn mǔankan. lûuk mǐi kɔ̂ phûut wâa,
'mii khray maa nâŋ thîi kâwʔîi nǔu mǔankan, lɛ́ɛw
kɔ̂ tham hàk dûay.

lɛ́ɛw phɔɔ mǐi, mɛ̂ɛ mǐi, lɛ́ʔ lûuk mǐi kɔ̂ deen
khâw pay duu nay hɔ̂ŋ nɔɔn. phɔɔ mǐi mɔɔŋ duu thîi
tiaŋ khɔ̌ŋ khâw lɛ́ɛw phûut sǐaŋ daŋ wâa, 'mii khray
maa nɔɔn thîi tiaŋ chǎn.' mɛ̂ɛ mǐi kɔ̂ phûut wâa,
'mii khray maa nɔɔn thîi tiaŋ chǎn mǔankan.' lûuk
mǐi kɔ̂ phûut wâa, 'mii khray maa nɔɔn thîi tiaŋ
nǔu mǔankan, lɛ́ɛw kɔ̂ kamlaŋ làp yùu dûay.' sǐaŋ
phûut khɔ̌ŋ lûuk mǐi daŋ mâak con tham hây cǔmcǐm
tɯ̀ɯn khɯ̂n maa. phɔɔ hěn wâa mii mǐi yùu nay bâan
kɔ̂ tòk cay mâak. rîip wîŋ ʔɔ̀ɔk càak bâan hǎay
pay. lɛ́ʔ tâŋtɛ̀ɛ nán maa, mǐi thaŋ sǎam tua nán
kɔ̂ mây day hěn dèk yǐŋ cǔmcǐm ʔìik lǝǝy.

41. THE SEVEN RARE IRREGULARS.

Practice copying the seven rare irregulars in the guidelines below. Use a ruler.

Now practice copying at normal handwriting size with guidelines but no ruler.

Now practice writing from memory. Proceed as with the corresponding exercise of lesson 1.

thɔɔ phûu thâw

tɔɔ patàk

thɔɔ monthoo

lɔɔ culaa

thɔ̌ɔ thǎan

chɔɔ kachəə

dɔɔ chadaa

44

42. DOUBLE-FUNCTIONING CONSONANTS.

Practice copying the common expressions given below (left). Then practice writing them from memory (right). Note mistakes in one column and then cover that column as you try again in the next.

วิทยุ			Radio.
พัทยา			Pataya.
ผลไม้			Fruit.
สกปรก			Dirty.
ศาสนา			Religion.
สุขภาพ			Health.
ตุ๊กตา			Doll.
สัตหีบ			Sattaheep.
อพยพ			To migrate.
รัฐบาล			The government.
ราชการ			Government service.
มัธยม			Secondary school.

45

43. IRREGULAR TONES.

Practice copying the expressions given below (left). Then practice writing them from memory (right).
Tones are shown in parentheses before each word.

(-ˋ)	ตำรวจ	Policeman.
(-ˋ)	ประโยชน์	Use.
(-–-ˊ)	ราชดำริ	Rajadamri Rd.
(-–-ˊ)	โฆษณา	Advertize.
(ˇ)	สำเร็จ	Succeed.
(-–-–-)	บุรุษไปรษณีย์	Postman.
(-ˊ)	สมาชิก	Member.
(-–-ˊ)	งานอดิเรก	Hobby.
(ˇ)	สำหรับ	For.
(ˇ)	ประโยค	Sentence.
(-–-)	สมาคม	Association.
(ˋ–-)	อิสลาม	Islam.
(-–-)	เพลงสวิง	Swing music.
(-ˋ)	อิสระ	Free.
(-ˋ)	เลขคณิต	Arithmetic.

46

(-ˇ) เบคอน	Bacon.
(ˇ) แบงก์	Bank.
(ˇ) กอล์ฟ	Golf.
(-ˊ) อพาร์ทเมนต์	Apartment.
(ˇˇ) พลาสติก	Plastic.
(-ˊ-) แอสไพริน	Aspirin.
(ˊ--) ออสเตรเลีย	Australia.
(ˇˇ) ออฟฟิศ	Office.
(ˇ) เทป	Tape.
(ˇ) แฟลต	Flat.
(-ˊ) ยุโรป	Europe.
(-ˊ-ˊ) เฟอร์นิเจอร์	Furniture.
(ˇˇ) ไนท์คลับ	Night club.
(-ˊ) นิวยอร์ก	New York.
(-ˇ) แครอท	Carrot.

44. MEANINGFUL TEXT. (*A got B from C.*)

Write the following questions and their answers in Thai.

Where did the government official go to get the radio?

....

Who went to get the plastic bags from the Association?

....

What did the bank manager go get from the post office?

....

Where did the policeman go to get the tape?

....

Who went to get the watch from the nightclub?

....

What did the air hostess go get from the bank?

....

Where did the advertiser go to get the furniture?

....

Who went to Sattaheep?

....

What did the postman go get from the nightclub.

....

Where did the Australian go to get the bacon?

....

Who went to get the golf clubs from Sattaheep?

....

What did the policeman go get from the supermarket?

....

Where did the cashier go to get the plastic bags?

....

Who went to get the furniture from Pataya?

....

What did the association member go get from Sattaheep?

....

Where did the cashier go?

....

Practice copying the following expressions (left). Then practice writing them from memory (right). Note mistakes in one column and then cover that column as you try again in the next.

ปั๊มน้ำมัน	……	……	……	A gas station.
ความสัมพันธ์	……	……	……	Relationship.
สมัย	……	……	……	Time, age, period.
ปลอดภัย	……	……	……	Safe.
มหาวิทยาลัย	……	……	……	University.
ภรรยา	……	……	……	Wife.
ตัวบรรจง	……	……	……	Block letters.
ไม้บรรทัด	……	……	……	Ruler.
ธรรมดา	……	……	……	Ordinary, common.
สรรพนาม	……	……	……	Pronoun.
วรรณยุกต์	……	……	……	Tone markers.
วรรค	……	……	……	Space between words.

49

46. IRREGULAR r'S.

Practice copying the following expressions (left). Then practice writing them from memory (right).
Note mistakes in one column and then cover that column as you try again in the next.

อังกฤษ			England.
จริง			True.
ทราบ			Know.
บริษัท			Company.
เสร็จ			Finish.
พฤษภา			May.
สามารถ			Able.
นคร			City.
สร้าง			Build.
รถจักรยาน			Bicycle.
อักษร			Letters.
บริเวณ			Area.
พฤศจิกา			November.
กระทรวง			Ministry.
ฤดู			Seasons.

50

47. IRREGULAR CLUSTERS AND VOWEL LENGTHS.

Most vowel length irregularities were covered in lessons 21 and 25 (shortenings of ee, εε, and ɔɔ; and lengthenings of ay and aw). The main point that remains is the shortening of aa in *weak-stressed* positions. All of the italicized a's in the following examples are written long: ʔathít, ʔeerɑwan, phɑsǎa, phayɑyaam, phayɑbaan, sǎalɑdeeŋ, rɑkhaa, mahǎawítthayɑlay, kɑŋkeeŋ, khâŋnâa, thân, mɑy malɑy. The last two, of course, are not examples of weak stress reduction. They are simply anomalies.

Practice copying the following expressions (left) and then writing them from memory (right).

อันตราย	......	Dangerous.
กรุณา	......	Please.
ปรอท	......	Thermometer.
กลาโหม	......	Ministry of Defense.
พฤหัส	......	Thursday.
พล	......	Power.
อาทิตย์	......	Week, Sunday.
พยายาม	......	Try.
ราคา	......	Price.
ข้างหน้า	......	In front of.
ท่าน	......	You.
ไม้มลาย	......	mɑy malɑy.

51

48. 'MEANINGFUL' TEXT. (*signs.*)

The following words (or word parts) are extremely common in signs. Practice copying them in the spaces to the left and then writing them from memory in the spaces to the right.

จำกัด			Limited.
ห้าง			Large store.
หุ้นส่วน			Partnership.
พาณิชย์			Commerce.
บริการ			Service.
สากล			Universal.
ชัย			Victory.
เลิศ			(excellence).
อุปกรณ์			Equipment.
รวม			United.
เจริญ			To advance.
พัฒนา			(develop).
ภัตตาคาร			Restaurant.
อาหาร			Food.
การค้า			Trading.

52

Write the following questions and their answers in Thai.

Who bought a vehicle
at the careen
sĭnsáp Company?

....

Where is the
wɔɔracàkyon
Company?

....

What company
sells trucks?

....

Who bought a vehicle
on săathɔɔn Road?

....

What kind of vehicle
did khun pradìt's
wife buy?

....

On what street did
khun prasèet's wife
buy a vehicle?

....

What company did
khun krìtsanăa buy
a vehicle from?

....

What kind of vehicle
does the company on
nakhɔɔn chaysĭi
Road sell?

....

Who bought a truck?

....

What kind of
vehicle does the
Asia Company sell?

....

Where is the company
that sells
bicycles?

....

Who bought a vehicle
on lŭaŋ Road?

....

Where is the
Asia Company?

....

What company
sells bicycles?

....

Who bought a vehicle
on nakhɔɔn chaysĭi
Road?

....

What kind of vehicle
does the company on
New phétburii Road
sell?

....

49. SILENT LETTERS.

Practice copying the following expressions (left) and then writing them from memory (right).

ชาติ			Nationality.
ภาพยนตร์			Movies.
ฟิล์ม			Film.
เหตุผล			Reason.
วิทยาศาสตร์			Science.
ภูมิใจ			To be proud.
ภูมิศาสตร์			Geography.
ต้นโพธิ์			The *bodh* tree.
รถเมล์			Bus.
พระพุทธ			The Buddha.
พราหมณ์			Brahmin.
วันจันทร์			Monday.
เกียรติ			Honor.
สวัสดิ์			Sawat (name).
ญาติ			Relatives.

50. UNWRITTEN VOWELS.

Practice copying the following expressions (left) and then writing them from memory (right).

ปกติ	....	Ordinarily.
กรณี	....	Circumstances.
สกปรก	....	Dirty.
สหรัฐ	....	United States.
จระเข้	....	Crocodile.
วรรณคดี	....	Literature.
นครปฐม	....	Province of Thailand.
สารคดี	....	Documentary.
จุฬาลงกรณ์	....	A Thai university.
บรรยาย	....	Lecture.
พฤหัสบดี	....	Thursday.
มนุษย์ชาติ	....	Mankind.
มาฆบูชา	....	A Buddhist holiday.
อนุสาวรีย์	....	Monument
ชัยสมรภูมิ	....	of Victory.

51. MODULATING WEAK SYLLABLES.

Practice copying the following expressions (left) and then writing them from memory (right).

ปรมาณู	....	Atom.
paramaanuu/parammanuu		
ศตวรรษ	....	Century.
sàttawát		
อมฤต	....	A brand of beer.
?ammarít		
วิศวกรรม	....	Engineering.
wísawakam		
ปฏิเสธ	....	To deny, refuse.
pàtiseet		
ปฏิกิริยา	....	Reaction.
patìkiriyaa		
คมนาคม	....	Communication.
khommanaakhom/khamanaakhom		
ธนบัตร	....	A banknote.
thonnabàt/thanabàt		
ประวัติ	....	A history.
prawàt		
ประวัติศาสตร์	....	The subject of History.
prawàttisàat		
กสิกร	....	Cultivated land.
kaseet		
กสิกรรม	....	The science of Agriculture.
kaseetsàat		

52. 'MEANINGFUL' TEXT. (Surnames.)

Write the following names. It is not expected, of course, that you should memorize the spellings, but being constantly forced to look them up will help you notice them better.

phannii kaancanarêak	....
wímon rí̓tthí̓kasêem	....
caruun klàtprawàt	....
yúphaa dìtsayanan	....
maalii klàttìsàksìi	....
sudaa phrommaalii	....
látdaa phoowíchian	....
yúphin niráttiphan	....
wílay ʔàtsawanon	....
cindaa dìtsoŋcan	....

ʔudom wátcharaaphɔɔnwíwát	....
cìttraa phaduŋsàttayawoŋ	....
wícìt ʔammarítwátthanakun	....
ʔuray rátchawɔɔraphoŋ	....
sawàt kìtìʔbunyaarátsamíi	....
suphót cìrakìtʔanusɔ̆ɔn	....
wíphaa cìraphoŋthanaawêet	....
chalɜ̆ɜm suphinthanaaphɔɔn	....
kìttìʔ hɔ̆ŋmaniiráttanakuun	....
ʔanoŋ thiirachaysùpphakìt	....

53. THAI NUMERALS.

Practice copying the Thai numerals in the guidelines below.

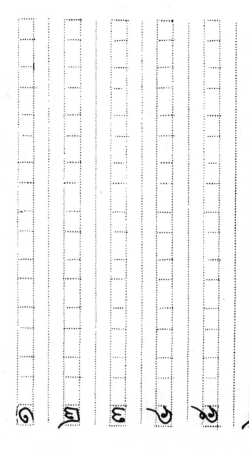

Now practice copying at normal handwriting size.

Now practice writing from memory. Simply write the Thai numerals after the Roman ones.

364	591	278	152
435	927	806	743
689	310	962	571
428	695	834	257
106	749	380	913

58

54. SUPPRESSED FINALS AND THEIR RESTORATION.

Transcriptions for the words in the text are given below for you to check your reading with. And meanings are given in case you're curious. You may want to try writing some of these words from memory, but more likely you will simply look each word up and copy it into its space. Most of these words are way above your present needs, and you are not expected to do any more with them than you want. The meanings of the word parts aren't given, but you will know some and be able to figure out others. Some of the more common suffixes are given below in case you're interested.

ความ Condition, state. วิทยา Science of -, -ology. การ Activity. ฏาร Field (of study). การ Matters. กร A worker.

khunprayòot	....	Usefulness.	sàkdinaa	Degrees of rank.
khunnaphâap	....	Quality.	canphen	Full moon.
sàt náam	....	Aquatic animal.	canthakhrâat / cantharakhrâat	Lunar eclipse.
sàttawaphêɛt	....	Veterinarian.	laaylák?àksɔ̌ɔn	Writing, script.
mítsǎmphan	....	Friendly relations.	láksanáanaam	Noun classifier.
míttraphâap	....	Friendship.	sawàtdiphâap	Well-being.
sǎan kheemii	....	Chemicals.	prasìtthiphâap	Efficiency.
sǎarakhadii	....	Documentary.	sǎmphanthaphâap	Relationship.
sàksìt	....	Sacred, inviolate.	sathǐanraphâap	Stability.

59

sǎnyaphêet	....	Surgeon.
phrúksachâat	....	The vegetable kingdom.
sǔunyaakàat	....	A vacuum.
kìattìsàk	....	Honor, prestige.
ʔàtthakhadìi	....	A law case.
ʔogkhamontrii	....	Privy councillor.
banphaburùt	....	Ancestors.
sàatsatraacaan	....	Professor.
phaanítchakaan phaanítchayakaan	....	Commerce.
kasàttarìyachâat	....	Military caste.
sǎnchâattayaan	....	Instinct.
khríttasàkàràt	....	Christian era.
wíwátthanaakaan	....	Evolution.

dunyaphâap dunlayaphâap	....	Equality.
sathǎapàttayakam	....	Architecture.
hàtthakam	....	Handicrafts.
kaayyakam	....	Gymnastics.
thammachâat	....	Nature.
thammasàat	....	Jurisprudence.
sèetthasàat	....	Economics.
sèetthakìt	....	Economy.
sèetthakaan	....	Economic matters.
sèetthakam	....	Economics.
rátthathammanuun	....	Constitution.
mâattrathǎan	....	Standard.
thantaphêet	....	Dentist.

60

55. MEANINGFUL TEXT. *(The Stubborn Pig.)*

Write the story from the transcription. Use extra paper as needed.

mǔu cɔɔm dɯ̄ɯ

naan maa lɛ́ɛw mii yǐŋ khon nɯŋ yùu nay bâan
lǎŋ lɛ́klɛ́k lǎŋ nɯŋ. tɔɔn cháaw wan nɯŋ khǎw kamlaŋ kwàat bâan yùu, khǎw phóp rían ŋen kàwkàw ʔan
nɯŋ. khǎw kèp rían nán wáy lɛ́ʔ khít ca ʔaw pay
sɯ́ɯ mǔu maa líaŋ. mɯ̂a tham ŋaan bâan sèt lɛ́ɛw,
khǎw cɯŋ rîip ʔɔ̀ɔk càak bâan pay, sɯ́ɯ mǔu. mɯ̂a
hǎy ŋen khon khǎay mǔu lɛ́ɛw, khǎw kɔ̂ phûut kàp
mǔu wâa, 'mǔu nɔ́ɔy, kradòot ʔɔ̀ɔk càak khɔ̂ɔk pay
kàp raw dǐawníi.' tɛ̀ɛ mǔu tua nán kɔ̂ mây yɔɔm.

yǐŋ nán cɯŋ dɤɤn pay hǎa mɯ̂a tua nɯŋ thîi yùu
klâyklây, lɛ́ɛw bɔ̀ɔk wâa, 'mɯ̂a nɔ́ɔy, chûay pay kàt
mǔu tua nán hây chán nɔ̀y ná. khǎw mây yɔɔm ʔɔ̀ɔk
càak khɔ̂ɔk pay kàp kap chán. thâa khǎw mây ʔɔ̀ɔk pay
khɯɯn níi, chán klàp bâan mây dâay nɛ̂nɛ̂.' mɯ̂a kɔ̂
tɔ̀ɔp wâa, 'chán kàt khǎw mây dâay lɔ̀k.'

càak khɔ̀ɔk pay kàp chán. thâa mǔu mây mây pay kàp
chán khɯɯn níi, chán klàp bâan mây dǎay nɛ̂nɛ̂.'
wua kɔ̌ bɔ̀ɔk wâa, 'chán dɯɯm nǎam mây dǎay lok.'

62

yǐŋ nán cɯŋ dɤɤn tɔ̀ɔ pay ʔìik kɔ̌ pay phóp mây-
thâaw ʔan nɯ̀ŋ. yǐŋ nán kɔ̌ bɔ̀ɔk máythâaw wâa,
'chɔ̀ay pay tii mǎa tua nán hây chán nɔ̀y. khǎw mây
yɔɔm pay kàt mǔu hây chán. mǔu kɔ̌ lɤɤy mây yɔɔm
ʔɔ̀ɔk càak khɔ̀ɔk pay kàp chán. thâa mǔu mây pay
kàp chán khɯɯn níi, chán klàp bâan mây dǎay nɛ̂nɛ̂.'
máythâaw kɔ̌ bɔ̀ɔk wâa, 'chán tii khǎw mây dǎay lok.'

yǐŋ nán cɯŋ dɤɤn tɔ̀ɔ pay ʔìik kɔ̌ pay phóp kɔɔŋ
fay kɔɔŋ nɯ̀ŋ. kɔ̌ bɔ̀ɔk kàp kɔɔŋ fay wâa. 'fay,
chɔ̀ay pay phǎw máythâaw ʔan nán hây chán nɔ̀y.
khǎw mây yɔɔm pay tii mǎa hây chán. mǎa kɔ̌ mây
yɔɔm pay kàt mǔu hây chán. mǔu kɔ̌ lɤɤy mây yɔɔm
ʔɔ̀ɔk càak khɔ̀ɔk pay kàp chán. thâa mǔu mây pay
kàp chán khɯɯn níi, chán klàp bâan mây dǎay nɛ̂nɛ̂.'
fay kɔ̌ bɔ̀ɔk wâa, 'chán phǎw khǎw mây dǎay lok.'

yǐŋ nán kɔ̌ dɤɤn tɔ̀ɔ pay ʔìik, phóp náam thâŋ
nɯ̌ŋ, kɔ̌ bɔ̀ɔk kàp náam wâa, 'náam, chɔ̀ay pay dàp
fay hây chán nɔ̀y. khǎw mây yɔɔm pay phǎw máythâaw hây chán. máythâaw kɔ̌ mây yɔɔm pay tii mǎa
hây chán. mǎa kɔ̌ mây yɔɔm pay kàt mǔu hây chán.
mǔu kɔ̌ lɤɤy mây yɔɔm ʔɔ̀ɔk càak khɔ̀ɔk pay kàp chán.
thâa mǔu mây pay kàp chán khɯɯn níi, chán klàp
bâan mây dǎay nɛ̂nɛ̂.' náam kɔ̌ bɔ̀ɔk wâa, 'chán dàp
fay mây dǎay lok.'

yǐŋ nán kɔ̌ dɤɤn tɔ̀ɔ pay ʔìik, phóp wua tua nɯ̀ŋ,
kɔ̌ bɔ̀ɔk kàp wua wâa, 'wua, chɔ̀ay pay dɯɯm náam nay
tháŋ hây chán nɔ̀y. khǎw mây yɔɔm dàp fay hây chán.
fay kɔ̌ mây yɔɔm phǎw máythâaw hây chán. máythâaw
kɔ̌ mây yɔɔm pay tii mǎa hây chán. mǎa kɔ̌ mây yɔɔm
pay kàt mǔu hây chán. mǔu kɔ̌ lɤɤy mây yɔɔm ʔɔ̀ɔk

56. MEANINGFUL TEXT. (The Stubborn Pig, continued.)

yǐŋ nán kɔ̂ dɛɛn tɔ̀ɔ pay ʔìik, phóp khon khǎa
sàt khon nɯŋ, kɔ̂ bɔ̀ɔk kàp kháw wâa, 'khon khǎa sàt,
chûay pay khǎa wua tua nán hây chán nɔ́y. kháw mây
yɔɔm kin naam hây chán. naam kɔ̂ mây yɔɔm pay dàp
fay hây chán. fay kɔ̂ mây yɔɔm pay phǎw máythǎaw
hây chán. máythǎaw kɔ̂ mây yɔɔm pay tii mǎa hây
chán. mǎa kɔ̂ mây yɔɔm pay kàt mǔu hây chán. mǔu
kɔ̂ lɛɛy mây yɔɔm ʔɔ̀ɔk càak khɔ̂ɔk pay kàp chán.
thâa mǔu mây pay kàp chán khɯɯn níi, chán klàp
bâan mây dâay nɛ́nɛ̂ɛ.' khon khǎa sàt bɔ̀ɔk wâa,
'chán khǎa khǎw mây dâay lok.'

yǐŋ nán kɔ̂ dɛɛn tɔ̀ɔ pay ʔìik, phóp chɯ̂ak sên
nɯŋ, kɔ̂ bɔ̀ɔk kàp chɯ̂ak wâa, 'chɯ̂ak, chûay pay
khwɛ̌ɛn khɔɔ khon khǎa sàt hây chán nɔ́y. kháw mây
yɔɔm pay khǎa wua hây chán. wua kɔ̂ mây yɔɔm pay
kin naam hây chán. naam kɔ̂ mây yɔɔm pay dàp fay
hây chán. fay kɔ̂ mây yɔɔm pay phǎw máythǎaw hây
chán. máythǎaw kɔ̂ mây yɔɔm pay tii mǎa hây chán.
mǎa kɔ̂ mây yɔɔm pay kàt mǔu hây chán. mǔu kɔ̂ lɛɛy
mây yɔɔm ʔɔ̀ɔk càak khɔ̂ɔk pay kàp chán. thâa mǔu
mây pay kàp chán khɯɯn níi, chán klàp bâan mây
dâay nɛ́nɛ̂ɛ.' chɯ̂ak kɔ̂ bɔ̀ɔk wâa, 'chán khwɛ̌ɛn khɔɔ
khǎw mây dâay lok.'

yǐŋ nán kɔ̂ dɛɛn tɔ̀ɔ pay ʔìik, phóp nǔu tua
nɯŋ, kɔ̂ bɔ̀ɔk kàp nǔu wâa, 'nǔu, chûay kàt chɯ̂ak
sên nán hây chán nɔ́y. kháw mây yɔɔm pay khwɛ̌ɛn
khɔɔ khon khǎa sàt hây chán. khon khǎa sàt kɔ̂ mây
yɔɔm pay khǎa wua hây chán. wua kɔ̂ mây yɔɔm pay
kin naam hây chán. naam kɔ̂ mây yɔɔm pay dàp fay

hây chán. fay kɔ̂ mây yɔɔm pay phǎw máythǎaw hây
chán. máythǎaw kɔ̂ mây yɔɔm pay tii mǎa hây chán.
mǎa kɔ̂ mây yɔɔm pay kàt mǔu hây chán. mǔu kɔ̂ lɛɛy
mây yɔɔm ʔɔ̀ɔk càak khɔ̂ɔk pay kàp chán. thâa mǔu
mây pay kàp chán khɯɯn níi, chán klàp bâan mây
dâay nɛ́nɛ̂ɛ.' nǔu kɔ̂ bɔ̀ɔk wâa, 'chán kàt chɯ̂ak mây
dâay lok.'

yǐŋ nán kɔ̂ dəən tɔ̀ɔ pay ʔìik, phóp mɛɛw tua
nʉ̀ŋ, kɔ̂ bɔ̀ɔk kàp mɛɛw wâa, 'mɛɛw, chûay pay kàt
nǔu hây chǎn nɔ̀y. khaw mây yɔɔm pay kàt chʉ̂ak hây
chǎn. chʉ̂ak kɔ̂ mây yɔɔm pay khwɛ̌ɛn khɔɔ khon khâa
sàt hây chǎn. khon khâa sàt kɔ̂ mây yɔɔm pay khâa
wua hây chǎn. wua kɔ̂ mây yɔɔm pay kin naam hây
chǎn. naam kɔ̂ mây yɔɔm pay dàp fay hây chǎn. fay
kɔ̂ mây yɔɔm pay phǎw máythâaw hây chǎn. máythâaw
kɔ̂ mây yɔɔm pay tii mǎa hây chǎn. mǎa kɔ̂ mây yɔɔm
pay kàt mǔu hây chǎn. mǔu kɔ̂ ləəy mây yɔɔm ʔɔ̀ɔk
caak khɔ̂ɔk pay kàp chǎn. thâa mǔu mây pay kàp
chǎn khʉʉn níi, chǎn klàp bâan mây dâay nɛ́nɛ̂.'
mɛɛw kɔ̂ bɔ̀ɔk kàp yǐŋ nán wâa, 'thâa pay ʔaw nom
mɛɛw kʉ̀ə wua thîi yùu thaaŋ nɔɔn maa hây chǎn dâay,
chǎn ca pay kàt nǔu hây.'

yǐŋ nán kɔ̂ rîip dəən pay hǎa mɛɛ wua tua nán
lɛ́ʔ phûut wâa, mɛɛ wua, khɔ̌ɔ nom hây chǎn sàk
thûay nʉ̀ŋ ná.' mɛɛ wua kɔ̂ tɔ̀ɔp wâa, 'thâa pay ʔaw
faaŋ maa hây chǎn kin dâay, chǎn ca hây nom khɔ̌ŋ
chǎn.' yǐŋ nán kɔ̂ rîip dəən pay ʔaw faaŋ maa hây
mɛɛ wua kin. mɛɛ mɛɛ wua kin ʔìm lɛɛw, kɔ̂ hây nom
khâw. yǐŋ nán rîip ʔaw nom pay hây mɛɛw kin.

mɛɛ mɛɛw kin ʔìm lɛɛw, kɔ̂ rîip wîŋ pay phʉ̂a ca
kàt nǔu. nǔu kɔ̂ rɔ́ɔŋ bɔ̀ɔk kàp mɛɛw wâa, 'yàa kàt
chǎn ləəy. chǎn ca pay kàt chʉ̂ak hây.' chʉ̂ak kɔ̂
rɔ́ɔŋ bɔ̀ɔk kàp nǔu wâa, 'yàa kàt chǎn ləəy. chǎn
ca khwɛ̌ɛn khɔɔ khon khâa sàt hây.' khon khâa sàt
kɔ̂ rɔ́ɔŋ bɔ̀ɔk kàp chʉ̂ak wâa, 'yàa khwɛ̌ɛn khɔɔ chǎn
ləəy. chǎn ca khâa wua hây.' wua kɔ̂ rɔ́ɔŋ bɔ̀ɔk
kàp khon khâa sàt wâa, 'yàa khâa chǎn ləəy. chǎn
ca kin naam hây.' naam kɔ̂ rɔ́ɔŋ bɔ̀ɔk kàp wua wâa,

'yàa kin chǎn ləəy. chǎn ca dàp fay hây.' fay kɔ̂
rɔ́ɔŋ bɔ̀ɔk kàp naam wâa, 'yàa dàp chǎn ləəy. chǎn
ca phǎw máythâaw hây.' máythâaw kɔ̂ rɔ́ɔŋ bɔ̀ɔk kàp
fay wâa, 'yàa phǎw chǎn ləəy. chǎn ca tii mǎa hây.'
mǎa kɔ̂ rɔ́ɔŋ bɔ̀ɔk kàp máythâaw wâa, 'yàa tii chǎn
ləəy. chǎn ca pay kàt mǔu hây.' lɛɛw kɔ̂ wîŋ khâw
pay ca kàt mǔu thîi yaŋ yùu nay khɔ̂ɔk. mǔu kɔ̂
rɔ́ɔŋ bɔ̀ɔk mǎa wâa, 'yàa kàt chǎn ləəy. chǎn ca
kradòot ʔɔ̀ɔk caak khɔ̂ɔk pay dîawníi la.' phɔɔ phûut lɛɛw,
mǔu kɔ̂ kradòot ʔɔ̀ɔk caak khɔ̂ɔk wîŋ pay hǎa yǐŋ khon
nán. lɛɛw kɔ̂ klàp bâan dûaykan nay wan nán ʔeeŋ.

....

....

....

....

....

57. REVIEW OF IRREGULARITIES.

Write the following examples of each irregularity type numbered below.

1. Kill, Friday, clock.   ....

2. Paper, sugar.   ....

3. Fruit, Pattaya   ....

4. Finished, meter.   ....

5. Car, telephone.   ....

6. Science of --,
   to have the right.   ....

7. Documentary, Maka Bucha.   ....

8. Sand, ministry.   ....

9. Dangerous,
   please (karunaa).   ....

10. Near, far.   ....

11. To suspect, gas station.   ....

12. Ruler, block letters.   ....

13. Pronoun, literature.   ....

14. Road, paper, U.S.   ....

15. Century, July.   ....

16. Morning, can,
    not (empty).   ....

17. University, price.   ....

18. Udorn, city.   ....

19. Area (bɔɔriween),
    crocodile.   ....

20. Thursday (full form).   ....

21. May, November, season.   ....

22. Reason, relatives.   ....

23. Easy, whisky.   ....

24. Kind of, want.   ....

25. Advertise, post office.   ....

26. Use(fulness), succeed.   ....

27. Apartment, flat.   ....

28. I (woman), ? (máy).   ....

29. Engineering, calendar.   ....

30. Book, kʰ.   ....

65

Write the following words with the help of irregularity numbers and necessary letters.

2 10 16 23 thít táay	19 2 4 bɔɔrimâat	23 1 4 23 nâasǎw
15 3 21 2 ʔammarít	1 15 2 3 13 2 sàttawát	12 4 2 sǎnsěen
14 29 1 2 22 pàtibàt	12 7 14 26 2 banphaburùt	2 30 3 4 2 5 phétchabuun
24 23 yàa yûŋ	1 7 20 raamaathíbɔdii	2 14 14 21 5 kaancanarɵ̂ek
19 2 6 bɔɔrisùt	26 2 5 prayòot	2 3 1 13 3 2 rátthathammanuun
1 3 9 2 sàkkaràat	29 7 29 wísǎakhàbuuchaa	4 2 3 1 6 kìattisàk
11 21 2 6 sǎmrít	21 1 14 2 22 phrúksachâat	14 2 3 17 11 mahǎawítthayalay
1 2 3 1 25 khɔ̌otsanaa	8 2 3 18 sàpphayaakɔɔn	1 4 2 1 14 1 2 6 sèetthasàat

66

58. REVIEW BY WORDS.

See how many of the following words you can spell correctly (on extra paper). Don't expect the English 'translations' to be accurate or complete. They are only intended to remind you of the Thai words on the corresponding page of the Text.

July	Mr. Mrs. Miss	know	service	History
circumstances	quality	you (up)	area	safe
paper	carrot	tape	company	gas station
ministry	advertise	telephone	pure	post office
Bangkok	hobby	bank note	baht	fruit
please	crocodile	bank (Thai)	postman	women
golf	true	nature	bacon	November
trade	Monday	ordinary	bank (English)	May
agriculture	limited	Thammasat	usually	Thursday
honor	progress	city	refuse	plastic
excuse me	victory	Nakhon Pathom	atom	Pattaya
thank you	nationality	Nakhon Sithammarat	thermometer	commerce
communication	relatives	sugar	democracy	Buddhist era
Christian era	block letters	New York	country	Wednesday
ought	police	night club	sentence	Phetchabun
relationship	doll	ancestors	use(fulness)	swing music

	máy malay			
film	may malay	radio	member	reasons
furniture	Europe	evolution	pronoun	monument
flat	bicycle	engineering	build	apartment
wife	bus	professor	well-being	office
restaurant	car	religion	hello	Australia
movies	constitution	Silapakorn	United States	letters
language	the government	Friday	veterinarian	liberal arts
proud	government service	vacuum	Sattaheep	English
geography	Rajadamri	economy	interview	Tuesday
food (eats)	Rajaprasong	economics	universal	dangerous
anthropology	season	dirty	able	might
university	classifier	to suspect	documentary	Southeast Asia
mathayom	characteristics	embassy	succeed	week, Sunday
Makha Bucha	arithmetic	architecture	health	food
standard	space between words	battlefield	Sukhumvit	free
friendship	literature	to apply	finish	Islam
have the right	tone markers	age, era	Saturday	industry
ruler	science	association	newspaper	aspirin

59. ALPHABETICAL ORDERING.

Alphabetize the words in each of the following groups by placing the appropriate order number in front of each word (the first word, for example, is the fifth of its group of seven words). You can check your ordering against the list of words on pages 67 and 68 of the Text.

60. VOCABULARY FOR THE LETTER.

The space to the right can be used for writing a letter of your own.

เรียน	To inform (a superior).	ดังนั้น	So, therefore.
เนื่องจาก	Owing to the fact that.	พนักงาน	Employee.
ข้าพเจ้า	khâaphacâw. I (very formal).	พร้อมทั้ง	Together with.
ประสงค์	Desire, need.	ระหว่าง	Between, during.
ท่าน	thân. You (very formal).	กำหนด	To fix a time.
ตกแต่ง	To decorate.	ดังกล่าว	As stated.
ส่วนตัว	Private, own.	แจ้ง	To inform, make known.
ณ	ná?. At, in.	เร็วๆนี้	In the near future.
สำนักงาน	Business office.	นับถือ	To respect.

60.1 LETTER. *(Form for addressing the envelope of a letter.)*

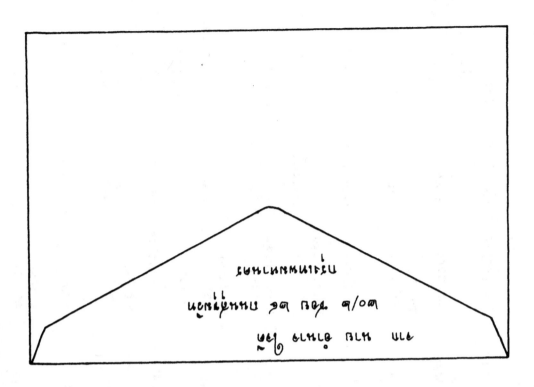

60.2 VOCABULARY FOR THE ESSAY.

หมู่บ้าน	Village.	นางพยาบาล	A nurse.	ประชาชน	The people.	สด	Fresh. ṣǎmrèt.
อำเภอ	Division of a caŋwat.	หน้าที่	Duty, function.	การโรง	Janitor.	สำเร็จ	To accomplish, be successful.
อำเภอเมือง	The capital ʔamphəə of a caŋwat.	ตรวจ	Examine, inspect.	สั่งสอน	Teach, admonish.	สำเร็จรูป	Ready-made.
เทศบาลตำบล	The capital city.	รักษา	To treat an illness.	เชื่อฟัง	To obey.	เครื่องครัว	Kitchen implements.
เจดีย์	Pagoda, stupa.	โรค	Sickness, disease.	กฎ	Rule, regulation.	เครื่องเรือน	Furniture.
พระพุทธรูป	Buddha image.	ฉีด	To inject, spray.	พระ	A buddhist monk.	สถานที่	Place, site.
มรรยาท	= มารยาท	จับ	To catch, grab, arrest.	วันพระ	Buddhist sabbath.	อาชีพ	Occupation.
เตียง	Bed.	ผิด	To be wrong.	ความสามัคคี	Harmony, unity, co-operation.	แตกต่าง	To differ, be different.
ไข้	Fever.	กฎหมาย	Law.	พ่อค้า	Merchant (man).	น้ำใจ	Good feelings, thoughtfulness.
คนไข้	Sick person, patient.	ลงโทษ	To punish.	แม่ค้า	Market woman.	ช่วยเหลือ	To help.
พยาบาล	To nurse, tend.	มิตร	mit. Friend.	ทำบุญ	To make merit.	ความสุข	Happiness.

60.3 VOCABULARY FOR THE PRATHOM 4 READING SELECTION.

ข้อความ	Reading passage.
จง	Imperative used in instructions.
ประวัติ	History.
เกิดมา	To occur, arise, come into being.
เกิดขึ้น	To happen.
อหิวาตกโรค	?ahíwaa takarôok. Cholera.
ล้ม	To fall, topple.
ตาย	To die.
จำนวน	Quantity, number, amount.
หมอ / หมอแพทย์	Doctor.
ป่วย	To be sick.
มักจะ	Likely to.
ดิบ	Raw, unripe, uncooked.
น้ำดิบ	Unboiled water.
ลำคลอง	Canal.
ใส่ใจ = ใส่ใจ	
เสียก่อน	Before.
แถบ	Region, zone.
วิธี	Method, way, means.
ชักจูง	Urge, persuade.
เอา	To take, bring.
ท้องถิ่น	Area, locality.
ปิ้ง	To heat by a fire.
เกรียม	Scorched, singed, parched.
เดือด	To be boiling.
ชง	To steep, make tea or coffee.
ทดลอง	To test, try out.
ชิม	To taste.
ใด	Which, what, any.
ฝาด	Astringent (puckering) taste.
ท้องร่วง	To have diarrhea.
กลิ่น	Odor.
ชวนดื่ม	Invite (make one want) to drink.
ดังนั้น	So.
ชาวบ้าน	Villagers, neighbors, common folk.
ป้องกัน	To prevent, protect.
พากัน	Acting together in like manner.
ติดใจ	To take a fancy to.
นิยม	To do by preference, favor, be popular.
สงบ	To become calm or quiet.
ซาลง	To subside, die down.
ประเพณี	Custom, tradition.
ปลูก	To plant.
แพร่หลาย	To spread out, be widespread.

60.4 VOCABULARY FOR THE NEWS ITEM.

กระจายเสียง	To broadcast.	ปฏิวัติ	To revolt.	แถลงการณ์	thaléɛŋkaan. Official announcement.	สำนักข่าว	News agency.
ข่าว	News.	ยึด	Capture, seize.	ชัยชนะ	Victory.	นายกรัฐมนตรี	Prime minister.
ด่วน	Urgent, express.	พร้อมกัน	Together with.	เนื่องจาก	Due to, arising from.	เลขาธิการ	Secretary general.
เมืองหลวง	Capital city.	เงื้อมมือ	Clutches, control.	สนับสนุน	To support.	พรรค	Political party.
กุมภา = เดือน	khamĕen. Cambodia.	ภายใต้	Under.	ท่วมท้น	To overflow.	รอง	Vice --, under --.
น. = นาฬิกา	O'clock (24 hr.).	นำ	To lead.	บรรดา	All.	รัฐมนตรี	ráttha-montrii. Minister.
ม.ค. = มกราคม	January.	บุก	To invade.	ประชาชน	The people.	ประมุข	Leader, chief.
สหภาพ	Union.	ศก	Year.	ชุด	Suit, set, team.	ประธาน	Chairman.
รอบ	Around, surrounding.	หัวหน้า	Leader, head.	โหดร้าย	To be cruel.	รัฐสภา	rátthasaphaa. Parliament.
กองทหาร	Army, troops.	คณะปฏิวัติ	Revolutionary party.	สังหาร	To kill.	กรรมการ	Committee member.
ฝ่าย	Side, group.	คณะ	Group, body.	ครองอำนาจ	To hold power.	ปักกิ่ง	Peking.

74

วิทยา	Biology.	เผา	To burn.	?attraa. อัตรา Ratio.	เปลี่ยนแปลง Change.
วิทยาศาสตร์ธรรมชาติ	"	ไฮโดรเจน	haydroocen. Hydrogen.	ปรมาณู	Atom.	sǎnyalák. สัญลักษณ์ Symbol.
แต่เดิม	Formerly.	ออกซิเจน	?ŏksicen. Oxygen.	ก๊าซ	Gas.	องค์ประกอบ Constituent part.
เชื่อว่า	It is believed.	เหลว	To be liquid.	ผสม	To mix.	daantân. ดาลตัน Dalton.
ธาตุ	Chemical element.	ใส	To be clear.	ปล่อย	To let loose.	thrít- sadii. ทฤษฎี Theory.
แยกออก	To separate.	ผล	Result.	กระแสไฟฟ้า	Electric current.	อะตอม Atom.
สาร	Substance.	ทดลอง	Experiment.	patìkiriyaa. ปฏิกิริยา Reaction.	โมเลกุล Molecule.
ข้อสังเกต	Observation.	ลำธาร	Stream.	ตายตัว	Fixed, invariable.	เช่นเดียวกัน The same as.
และ	To suggest.	เคมี	Chemistry.	รวม	To combine with.	แตกต่าง To differ.
สำประกอบ	Compound.	นักเคมี	Chemist.	ระเบิด	To explode.	ข้อแตกต่าง Differ- ence.
เกิดขึ้น	To happen.	ประกอบด้วย	Composed of.	เพียง	Only.	อนุภาค Factor, atom.

75

60.6 VOCABULARY FOR THE SOCIAL SCIENCE PASSAGE.

ชาวเขา	Mountain people.
เกิดขึ้น	Come into being.
ถ้าหาก	If.
เพ่งพิจารณา	phícaaranaa. To consider.
ระยะ	Interval of space or time.
อพยพ	ʔòpphayóp. To migrate.
ได้แก่	To live, dwell.
แบ่ง	To divide.
ภาค	Part, section, region.
เหนือ	North, above.
พวก	Group.
แนวคิด	Nation-ality.
ภูมิภาค	Region.
ตะวันออก	East.
เฉียง	Diagonal.
ใต้	tâay. South, under.
ตะวันออกเฉียงใต้	South-east.
ได้แก่	To consist of.
ยุค	Period, duration.
ศตวรรษ	sàttawát. Century.
การก	Lineage, ancestry.
ทิเบต-พม่า	Tibeto-Burman.
เดิม	Former previous.
ไทยน้อย	The Thais of Thailand.
ไทยใหญ่	Shans (Thais of Burma).
อาคเนย์	ʔaakhanee. Southeast.
ถิ่น	Locality.
มอญ-เขมร	Mon-Khmer.
ดังกล่าว	As said before.
กลืน	To swallow.
หลบหนี	To avoid, escape.
ป่า	Jungle, forest.
ชน	People.
สืบ	To pass on.
เชื้อ	Family line.
เชื้อสาย	Lineage.
สืบเชื้อสาย	To continue the lineage.
นัย, นัยยะ	nay, nayya. Way of explaining.
ผ่าน	To pass (time).
ภายหลัง	After.
อิทธิพล	Influence.
คุณสมบัติ	khunnasŏmbàt. Qualities, property.
คล้ายคลึง	To be similar.
ไพร่	= People.

60.7 VOCABULARY FOR THE ANNOUNCEMENT.

อาคาร	A building.	ประธาน	Chairman.	เดิม	Originally.	ประกอบกับ	Together with.
พิธี	Ceremony.	งบประมาณ	Budget.	เจ้าหน้าที่	Official.	คณะ	A group or body.
ป้าย	Poster, sign, label.	แผ่นดิน	Nation, realm, reign.	ปฏิบัติ pàtibàt. To perform.	บริหาร	To administer.
หน่วยงาน	Government office.	ในวงเงิน	Within the amount of.	ระเบียง	Porch, veranda.	กิจการ	kìtcakaan. Business, activity. ส่งเสริม sòŋ sěem.
ด้าน	Side.	เหลี่ยม	Area.	แก่	To, for.	ส่งเสริม	To encourage, promote.
หอสมุด	Library.	การางเมตร taraaŋ méet. Sq. meters.	ประสิทธิภาพ	Efficiency.	เผยแพร่	To spread out, popularize.
แห่งชาติ	National.	แบ่ง	To divide.	อีกทั้ง	Furthermore.	สรรพวิชา	sàpph-. Various kinds of knowledge.
เดิม	Original, former.	แบ่งเบา...ลง	To lessen, lighten.	ขยาย	To enlarge.	คุณประโยชน์	Usefulness, value.
พลตรี	Major General.	แออัด	Congested, crowded.	โครงการ	Project, program.	ประเทศชาติ	Country.
เสด็จ	To go (royal lang.).	ยัดเยียด	Stuffed, crowded.	วางไว้	To place, arrange, stipulate.	ประชาชน	The people.
องค์	Classifier for royal personages.	สถานที่	Place, site.	หวัง	To hope.	การพัฒนา	To progress, advance, develop.

60.8 VOCABULARY FOR THE FICTION PASSAGE.

ชีวิต	Life.	อาชีพ	Occupation.	บุคคล	bùkkhon. Person, individual.	ใด	What, which any.
หมู่	Group.	แต่ละ	tɛla, tala. Each and every.	เหตุใด	hèet chanǎy. For what reason.	บันดาล	To produce or cause (super-naturally).
หนุ่ม	Young man.	ทุกข์	Suffering, unhappiness.	สิ้นสุด	To terminate.	ผล	Result.
วัย	Period of life.	สุข	Happiness.	เหตุ	hèet. Cause, reason.	สนอง	Give in recompense or retribution.
ชรา	Old aged.	ทรมาน	thɔɔramaan. To torture.	สถาน	Place, site.	ตอบแทน	To return a favor, repay.
คหบดี	khàʔbɔdii. Rich man.	สิ้น	Come to an end.	มากมาย	= มาก	ความชั่ว	Evils, vice.
มั่งมี	Rich, prosperous.	ร่วมกับ	To join together.	ประสบ	To meet, encounter.	ปรารถนา	pràatthanǎa. To desire, wish.
ไร่	Plantation farm, field.	ประกอบ	To do, perform.	เคราะห์	Bad luck, fate.	มิฉะนั้น = มิเช่นนั้น	Otherwise.
สมณะ	samaná?. Buddhist monk.	กรรม	Karma, one's deeds (usually bad).	จมเจ่า	To sink.	จุดจบ	The ending point.
วัย	Period of life.	ทั้งสิ้น	Entirely.	ซึ่ง	That, which.	ประโยคชีวิต	The 'sentence' of life.
เพศ	Sex.	สุดแต่ว่า	Depending on.	ร้ายแรง	Severe, serious.	ยืดยาว	Long, extensive.

78

This page can be used for the 'additional practice' of the next few lessons.

H1. (handwriting samples)

Four different handwriting samples of each of the seven letters are given below (2 women's at the left and 2 men's at the right). For each sample, first *imagine* yourself *boldly* writing the three letters, and then use this *feeling* to guide you as you repeatedly write the letter in the space following the sample. The suggested process is one of *feeling*, not *copying*. Pick the sample that *feels* best to you and practice it on additional paper.

H2.

Develop and practice your handwriting of these seven letters as suggested on page W80.

H3. ຄ ຄ ຄ ຄ ຄ ຄ ຄ .

Develop and practice your handwriting of these seven letters as suggested on page W80.

82

H4. อ ฮ ว ร ย จ ง .

Develop and practice your handwriting of these seven letters as suggested on page W80.

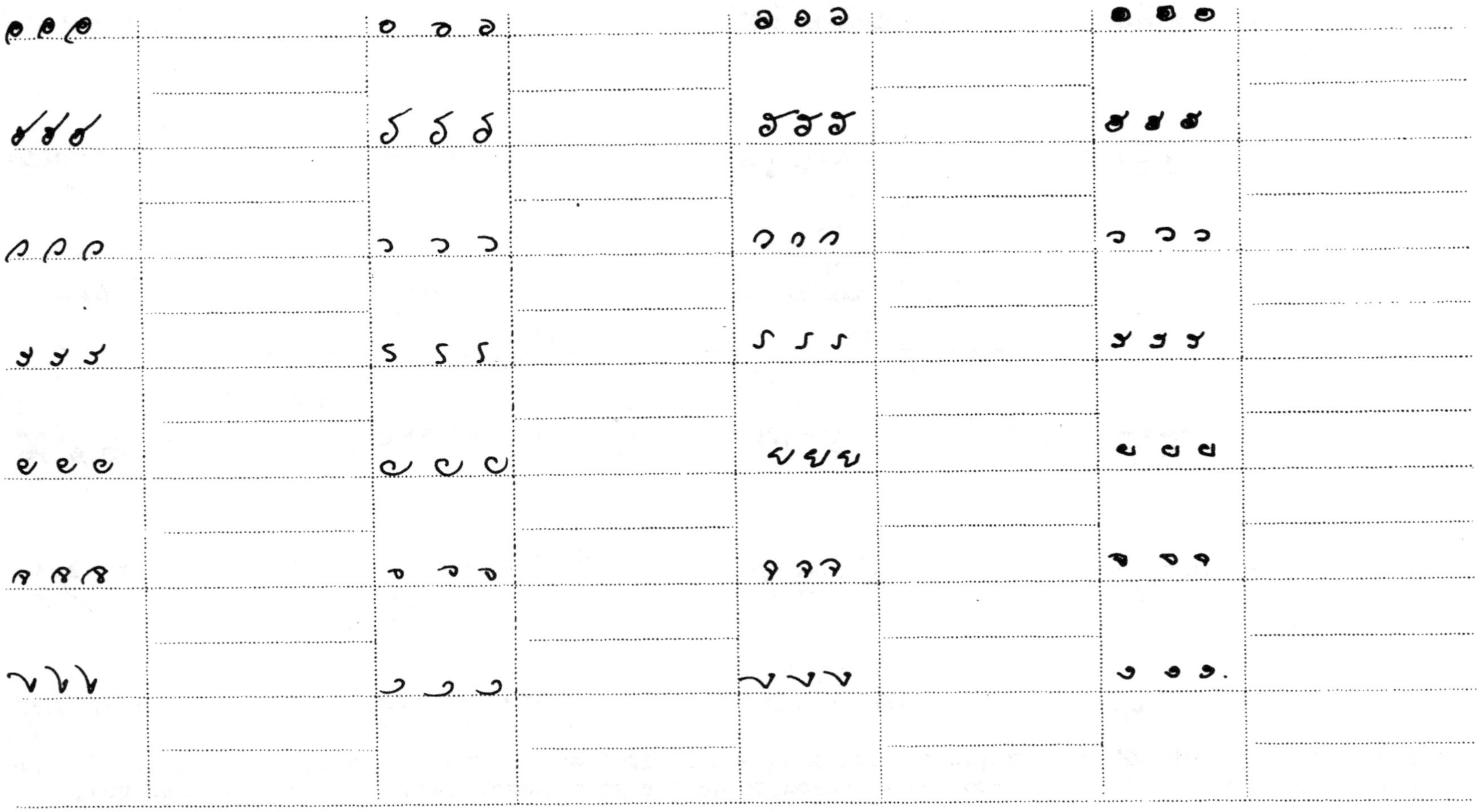

H5.   ˊ -   ˇ   -   ˙   -   ˆ   -ː -ːˈ -ˌ   .

Each phrase below has three examples of a tone or vowel symbol and is given in 4 different hand-writings as before. Practice each phrase just as you have been practicing the groups of 3 consonants.

H6.

Develop and practice your handwriting of these vowels as suggested on page W84.

H7.

Develop and practice your handwriting of these vowels as suggested on page W84.

86

H8.

Develop and practice your handwriting of these symbols as suggested on page W84.

H9. TWENTY SAMPLES. Practice writing any of the 20 handwritings that appeal to you.

88

89

91

H10.

Develop and practice your handwriting of these seven letters as suggested on page W80.

H11.

Develop and practice your handwriting of these seven letters as suggested on page W80.

93

SOUTHEAST ASIA PROGRAM PUBLICATIONS

Cornell University

Studies on Southeast Asia

Number 30   *Violence and the State in Suharto's Indonesia,* ed. Benedict R. O'G. Anderson. 2001. 247 pp. ISBN 0-87727-729-X

Number 29   *Studies in Southeast Asian Art: Essays in Honor of Stanley J. O'Connor,* ed. Nora A. Taylor. 2000. 243 pp. Illustrations. ISBN 0-87727-728-1

Number 28   *The Hadrami Awakening: Community and Identity in the Netherlands East Indies, 1900-1942,* Natalie Mobini-Kesheh. 1999. 174 pp. ISBN 0-87727-727-3

Number 27   *Tales from Djakarta: Caricatures of Circumstances and their Human Beings,* Pramoedya Ananta Toer. 1999. 145 pp. ISBN 0-87727-726-5

Number 26   *History, Culture, and Region in Southeast Asian Perspectives,* rev. ed., O. W. Wolters. 1999. 275 pp. ISBN 0-87727-725-7

Number 25   *Figures of Criminality in Indonesia, the Philippines, and Colonial Vietnam,* ed. Vicente L. Rafael. 1999. 259 pp. ISBN 0-87727-724-9

Number 24   *Paths to Conflagration: Fifty Years of Diplomacy and Warfare in Laos, Thailand, and Vietnam, 1778-1828,* Mayoury Ngaosyvathn and Pheuiphanh Ngaosyvathn. 1998. 268 pp. ISBN 0-87727-723-0

Number 23   *Nguyễn Cochinchina: Southern Vietnam in the Seventeenth and Eighteenth Centuriess,* Li Tana. 1998. 194 pp. ISBN 0-87727-722-2

Number 22   *Young Heroes: The Indonesian Family in Politics,* Saya S. Shiraishi. 1997. 183 pp. ISBN 0-87727-721-4

Number 21   *Interpreting Development: Capitalism, Democracy, and the Middle Class in Thailand,* John Girling. 1996. 95 pp. ISBN 0-87727-720-6

Number 20   *Making Indonesia,* ed. Daniel S. Lev, Ruth McVey. 1996. 201 pp. ISBN 0-87727-719-2

Number 19   *Essays into Vietnamese Pasts,* ed. K. W. Taylor, John K. Whitmore. 1995. 288 pp. ISBN 0-87727-718-4

Number 18   *In the Land of Lady White Blood: Southern Thailand and the Meaning of History,* Lorraine M. Gesick. 1995. 106 pp. ISBN 0-87727-717-6

Number 17   *The Vernacular Press and the Emergence of Modern Indonesian Consciousness,* Ahmat Adam. 1995. 220 pp. ISBN 0-87727-716-8

Number 16   *The Nan Chronicle,* trans., ed. David K. Wyatt. 1994. 158 pp. ISBN 0-87727-715-X

Number 15   *Selective Judicial Competence: The Cirebon-Priangan Legal Administration, 1680–1792,* Mason C. Hoadley. 1994. 185 pp. ISBN 0-87727-714-1

Number 14   *Sjahrir: Politics and Exile in Indonesia,* Rudolf Mrázek. 1994. 536 pp. ISBN 0-87727-713-3

Number 13   *Fair Land Sarawak: Some Recollections of an Expatriate Officer,* Alastair Morrison. 1993. 196 pp. ISBN 0-87727-712-5

Number 12   *Fields from the Sea: Chinese Junk Trade with Siam during the Late Eighteenth and Early Nineteenth Centuries,* Jennifer Cushman. 1993. 206 pp. ISBN 0-87727-711-7

Number 11   *Money, Markets, and Trade in Early Southeast Asia: The Development of Indigenous Monetary Systems to AD 1400*, Robert S. Wicks. 1992. 2nd printing 1996. 354 pp., 78 tables, illus., maps. ISBN 0-87727-710-9

Number 10   *Tai Ahoms and the Stars: Three Ritual Texts to Ward Off Danger*, trans., ed. B. J. Terwiel, Ranoo Wichasin. 1992. 170 pp. ISBN 0-87727-709-5

Number 9   *Southeast Asian Capitalists*, ed. Ruth McVey. 1992. 2nd printing 1993. 220 pp. ISBN 0-87727-708-7

Number 8   *The Politics of Colonial Exploitation: Java, the Dutch, and the Cultivation System*, Cornelis Fasseur, ed. R. E. Elson, trans. R. E. Elson, Ary Kraal. 1992. 2nd printing 1994. 266 pp. ISBN 0-87727-707-9

Number 7   *A Malay Frontier: Unity and Duality in a Sumatran Kingdom*, Jane Drakard. 1990. 215 pp. ISBN 0-87727-706-0

Number 6   *Trends in Khmer Art*, Jean Boisselier, ed. Natasha Eilenberg, trans. Natasha Eilenberg, Melvin Elliott. 1989. 124 pp., 24 plates. ISBN 0-87727-705-2

Number 5   *Southeast Asian Ephemeris: Solar and Planetary Positions, A.D. 638–2000*, J. C. Eade. 1989. 175 pp. ISBN 0-87727-704-4

Number 3   *Thai Radical Discourse: The Real Face of Thai Feudalism Today*, Craig J. Reynolds. 1987. 2nd printing 1994. 186 pp. ISBN 0-87727-702-8

Number 1   *The Symbolism of the Stupa*, Adrian Snodgrass. 1985. Revised with index, 1988. 3rd printing 1998. 469 pp. ISBN 0-87727-700-1

SEAP Series

Number 18   *Culture and Power in Traditional Siamese Government*, Neil A. Englehart. 2001. 130 pp. ISBN 0-87727-135-6

Number 17   *Gangsters, Democracy, and the State*, ed. Carl A. Trocki. 1998. 94 pp. ISBN 0-87727-134-8

Number 16   *Cutting Across the Lands: An Annotated Bibliography on Natural Resource Management and Community Development in Indonesia, the Philippines, and Malaysia*, ed. Eveline Ferretti. 1997. 329 pp. ISBN 0-87727-133-X

Number 15   *The Revolution Falters: The Left in Philippine Politics After 1986*, ed. Patricio N. Abinales. 1996. 182 pp. ISBN 0-87727-132-1

Number 14   *Being Kammu: My Village, My Life*, ed. Damrong Tayanin. 1994. 138 pp., 22 tables, illus., maps. ISBN 0-87727-130-5

Number 13   *The American War in Vietnam*, ed. Jayne Werner, David Hunt. 1993. 132 pp. ISBN 0-87727-131-3

Number 12   *The Political Legacy of Aung San*, ed. Josef Silverstein. Revised edition 1993. 169 pp. ISBN 0-87727-128-3

Number 10   *Studies on Vietnamese Language and Literature: A Preliminary Bibliography*, Nguyen Dinh Tham. 1992. 227 pp. ISBN 0-87727-127-5

Number 9   *A Secret Past*, Dokmaisot, trans. Ted Strehlow. 1992. 2nd printing 1997. 72 pp. ISBN 0-87727-126-7

Number 8   *From PKI to the Comintern, 1924–1941: The Apprenticeship of the Malayan Communist Party*, Cheah Boon Kheng. 1992. 147 pp. ISBN 0-87727-125-9

Number 7   *Intellectual Property and US Relations with Indonesia, Malaysia, Singapore, and Thailand*, Elisabeth Uphoff. 1991. 67 pp. ISBN 0-87727-124-0

Number 6   *The Rise and Fall of the Communist Party of Burma (CPB)*, Bertil Lintner. 1990. 124 pp. 26 illus., 14 maps. ISBN 0-87727-123-2

Number 5   *Japanese Relations with Vietnam: 1951–1987*, Masaya Shiraishi. 1990. 174 pp. ISBN 0-87727-122-4

Number 3   *Postwar Vietnam: Dilemmas in Socialist Development*, ed. Christine White, David Marr. 1988. 2nd printing 1993. 260 pp. ISBN 0-87727-120-8

Number 2   *The Dobama Movement in Burma (1930–1938)*, Khin Yi. 1988. 160 pp. ISBN 0-87727-118-6

Translation Series

Volume 4   *Approaching Suharto's Indonesia from the Margins*, ed. Takashi Shiraishi. 1994. 153 pp. ISBN 0-87727-403-7

Volume 3   *The Japanese in Colonial Southeast Asia*, ed. Saya Shiraishi, Takashi Shiraishi. 1993. 172 pp. ISBN 0-87727-402-9

Volume 2   *Indochina in the 1940s and 1950s*, ed. Takashi Shiraishi, Motoo Furuta. 1992. 196 pp. ISBN 0-87727-401-0

Volume 1   *Reading Southeast Asia*, ed. Takashi Shiraishi. 1990. 188 pp. ISBN 0-87727-400-2

CORNELL MODERN INDONESIA PROJECT PUBLICATIONS

Cornell University

Number 75   *A Tour of Duty: Changing Patterns of Military Politics in Indonesia in the 1990s.* Douglas Kammen and Siddharth Chandra. 1999. 99 pp. ISBN 0-87763-049-6

Number 74   *The Roots of Acehnese Rebellion 1989–1992*, Tim Kell. 1995. 103 pp. ISBN 0-87763-040-2

Number 73   *"White Book" on the 1992 General Election in Indonesia*, trans. Dwight King. 1994. 72 pp. ISBN 0-87763-039-9

Number 72   *Popular Indonesian Literature of the Qur'an*, Howard M. Federspiel. 1994. 170 pp. ISBN 0-87763-038-0

Number 71   *A Javanese Memoir of Sumatra, 1945–1946: Love and Hatred in the Liberation War*, Takao Fusayama. 1993. 150 pp. ISBN 0-87763-037-2

Number 70   *East Kalimantan: The Decline of a Commercial Aristocracy*, Burhan Magenda. 1991. 120 pp. ISBN 0-87763-036-4

Number 69   *The Road to Madiun: The Indonesian Communist Uprising of 1948*, Elizabeth Ann Swift. 1989. 120 pp. ISBN 0-87763-035-6

Number 68   *Intellectuals and Nationalism in Indonesia: A Study of the Following Recruited by Sutan Sjahrir in Occupation Jakarta*, J. D. Legge. 1988. 159 pp. ISBN 0-87763-034-8

Number 67 *Indonesia Free: A Biography of Mohammad Hatta*, Mavis Rose. 1987. 252 pp. ISBN 0-87763-033-X

Number 66 *Prisoners at Kota Cane*, Leon Salim, trans. Audrey Kahin. 1986. 112 pp. ISBN 0-87763-032-1

Number 65 *The Kenpeitai in Java and Sumatra*, trans. Barbara G. Shimer, Guy Hobbs, intro. Theodore Friend. 1986. 80 pp. ISBN 0-87763-031-3

Number 64 *Suharto and His Generals: Indonesia's Military Politics, 1975–1983*, David Jenkins. 1984. 4th printing 1997. 300 pp. ISBN 0-87763-030-5

Number 62 *Interpreting Indonesian Politics: Thirteen Contributions to the Debate, 1964–1981*, ed. Benedict Anderson, Audrey Kahin, intro. Daniel S. Lev. 1982. 3rd printing 1991. 172 pp. ISBN 0-87763-028-3

Number 61 *Sickle and Crescent: The Communist Revolt of 1926 in Banten*, Michael C. Williams. 1982. 81 pp. ISBN 0-87763-027-5

Number 60 *The Minangkabau Response to Dutch Colonial Rule in the Nineteenth Century*, Elizabeth E. Graves. 1981. 157 pp. ISBN 0-87763-000-3

Number 59 *Breaking the Chains of Oppression of the Indonesian People: Defense Statement at His Trial on Charges of Insulting the Head of State, Bandung, June 7–10, 1979*, Heri Akhmadi. 1981. 201 pp. ISBN 0-87763-001-1

Number 58 *Administration of Islam in Indonesia*, Deliar Noer. 1978. 82 pp. ISBN 0-87763-002-X

Number 57 *Permesta: Half a Rebellion*, Barbara S. Harvey. 1977. 174 pp. ISBN 0-87763-003-8

Number 55 *Report from Banaran: The Story of the Experiences of a Soldier during the War of Independence*, Maj. Gen. T. B. Simatupang. 1972. 186 pp. ISBN 0-87763-005-4

Number 52 *A Preliminary Analysis of the October 1 1965, Coup in Indonesia (Prepared in January 1966)*, Benedict R. Anderson, Ruth T. McVey, assist. Frederick P. Bunnell. 1971. 3rd printing 1990. 174 pp. ISBN 0-87763-008-9

Number 51 *The Putera Reports: Problems in Indonesian-Japanese War-Time Cooperation*, Mohammad Hatta, trans., intro. William H. Frederick. 1971. 114 pp. ISBN 0-87763-009-7

Number 50 *Schools and Politics: The Kaum Muda Movement in West Sumatra (1927–1933)*, Taufik Abdullah. 1971. 257 pp. ISBN 0-87763-010-0

Number 49 *The Foundation of the Partai Muslimin Indonesia*, K. E. Ward. 1970. 75 pp. ISBN 0-87763-011-9

Number 48 *Nationalism, Islam and Marxism*, Soekarno, intro. Ruth T. McVey. 1970. 2nd printing 1984. 62 pp. ISBN 0-87763-012-7

Number 43 *State and Statecraft in Old Java: A Study of the Later Mataram Period, 16th to 19th Century*, Soemarsaid Moertono. Revised edition 1981. 180 pp. ISBN 0-87763-017-8

Number 37 *Mythology and the Tolerance of the Javanese*, Benedict R. O'G. Anderson. 2nd edition 1997. 104 pp., 65 illus. ISBN 0-87763-041-0

Number 25 *The Communist Uprisings of 1926–1927 in Indonesia: Key Documents*, ed., intro. Harry J. Benda, Ruth T. McVey. 1960. 2nd printing 1969. 177 pp. ISBN 0-87763-024-0

Number   7   *The Soviet View of the Indonesian Revolution*, Ruth T. McVey. 1957. 3rd printing 1969. 90 pp.
ISBN 0-87763-018-6

Number   6   *The Indonesian Elections of 1955*, Herbert Feith. 1957. 2nd printing 1971. 91 pp. ISBN 0-87763-020-8

LANGUAGE TEXTS

INDONESIAN

Beginning Indonesian Through Self-Instruction, John U. Wolff, Dédé Oetomo, Daniel Fietkiewicz. 3rd revised edition 1992. 3 volume set. 1,057 pp.
ISBN 0-87727-519-X

Indonesian Readings, John U. Wolff. 1978. 4th printing 1992. 480 pp.
ISBN 0-87727-517-3

Indonesian Conversations, John U. Wolff. 1978. 3rd printing 1991. 297 pp.
ISBN 0-87727-516-5

Formal Indonesian, John U. Wolff. 2nd revised edition 1986. 446 pp.
ISBN 0-87727-515-7

TAGALOG

Pilipino Through Self-Instruction, John U. Wolff, Ma. Theresa C. Centano, Der-Hwa U. Rau. 1991. 4 volume set. 1,490 pp. ISBN 0-87727-524-6

THAI

A. U. A. Language Center Thai Course Book 1, J. Marvin Brown. Originally published by the American University Alumni Association Language Center, 1974. Reissued by Cornell Southeast Asia Program,1991. 267 pp. ISBN 0-87727-506-8

A. U. A. Language Center Thai Course Book 2, 1992. 288 pp. ISBN 0-87727-507-6

A. U. A. Language Center Thai Course Book 3, 1992. 247 pp. ISBN 0-87727-508-4

A. U. A. Language Center Thai Course, Reading and Writing Text (mostly reading), 1979. Reissued 1997. 164 pp. ISBN 0-87727-511-4

A. U. A. Language Center Thai Course, Reading and Writing Workbook (mostly writing), 1979. Reissued 1997. 99 pp. ISBN 0-87727-512-2

KHMER

Cambodian System of Writing and Beginning Reader, Franklin E. Huffman. Originally published by Yale University Press, 1970. Reissued by Cornell Southeast Asia Program, 3rd printing 1992. 365 pp. ISBN 0-300-01314-0

Modern Spoken Cambodian, Franklin E. Huffman, assist. Charan Promchan, Chhom-Rak Thong Lambert. Originally published by Yale University Press, 1970. Reissued by Cornell Southeast Asia Program, 3rd printing 1991. 451 pp. ISBN 0-300-01316-7

Intermediate Cambodian Reader, ed. Franklin E. Huffman, assist. Im Proum. Originally published by Yale University Press, 1972. Reissued by Cornell Southeast Asia Program, 1988. 499 pp. ISBN 0-300-01552-6

Cambodian Literary Reader and Glossary, Franklin E. Huffman, Im Proum. Originally published by Yale University Press, 1977. Reissued by Cornell Southeast Asia Program, 1988. 494 pp. ISBN 0-300-02069-4

HMONG

White Hmong-English Dictionary, Ernest E. Heimbach. 1969. 7th printing 1997. 523 pp. ISBN 0-87727-075-9

VIETNAMESE

Intermediate Spoken Vietnamese, Franklin E. Huffman, Tran Trong Hai. 1980. 3rd printing 1994. ISBN 0-87727-500-9

* * *

Southeast Asian Studies: Reorientations. Craig J. Reynolds and Ruth McVey. Frank H. Golay Lectures 2 & 3. 70 pp. ISBN 0-87727-301-4

Javanese Literature in Surakarta Manuscripts, Nancy K. Florida. Hard cover series ISBN 0-87727-600-5; Paperback series ISBN 0-87727-601-3. Vol. 1, *Introduction and Manuscripts of the Karaton Surakarta*. 1993. 410 pp. Frontispiece, 5 illus. Hard cover, ISBN 0-87727-602-1, Paperback, ISBN 0-87727-603-X

Sbek Thom: Khmer Shadow Theater. Pech Tum Kravel, trans. Sos Kem, ed. Thavro Phim, Sos Kem, Martin Hatch. 1996. 363 pp., 153 photographs. ISBN 0-87727-620-X

In the Mirror, Literature and Politics in Siam in the American Era, ed. Benedict R. O'G. Anderson, trans. Benedict R. O'G. Anderson, Ruchira Mendiones. 1985. 2nd printing 1991. 303 pp. Paperback. ISBN 974-210-380-1

To order, please contact:

Cornell University
SEAP Distribution Center
369 Pine Tree Rd.
Ithaca, NY 14850-2819 USA

Tel: 1-877-865-2432 (Toll free – U.S.)
Fax: (607) 255-7534

E-mail: SEAP-Pubs@cornell.edu

Orders must be prepaid by check or credit card (VISA, MasterCard, Discover).